TEST CONSTRUCTION FOR TRAINING EVALUATION

Van Nostrand Reinhold/American Society for Training and Development Series

Selecting and Developing Media for Instruction, by *Ronald H. Anderson*
Test Construction for Training Evaluation, by *Charles C. Denova*
Guidebook for International Trainers in Business and Industry, by *Vincent A. Miller*

TEST CONSTRUCTION FOR TRAINING EVALUATION

Charles C. Denova

American Society for Training and Development
Madison, Wisconsin

VNR VAN NOSTRAND REINHOLD COMPANY

NEW YORK   CINCINNATI   ATLANTA   DALLAS   SAN FRANCISCO
LONDON   TORONTO   MELBOURNE

Van Nostrand Reinhold Company Regional Offices:
New York Cincinnati Atlanta Dallas San Francisco

Van Nostrand Reinhold Company International Offices:
London Toronto Melbourne

Library of Congress Catalog Card Number: 78-26350
ISBN: 0-442-22073-1

Manufactured in the United States of America

Published by Van Nostrand Reinhold Company
135 West 50th Street, New York, N.Y. 10020
and
American Society for Training and Development
P.O. Box 5307, Madison, Wisconsin 53705

Published simultaneously in Canada by Van Nostrand Reinhold Ltd.

15 14 13 12 11 10 9 8 7 6 5 4 3 2 1

Library of Congress Cataloging in Publication Data

Denova, Charles C   1928-
  Test construction for training evaluation.

  Includes index.
  1. Educational tests and measurements. I. Title.
LB3051.D44   371.2′61   78-26350
ISBN 0-442-22073-1

To
Charlene, Bruce, and Keith,
who are constantly testing me as a parent, and to
Sam J. D'Amico,
who has always been my standard of measure.

Preface

Instructors in business and industry often approach testing and evaluation reluctantly. Yet, without a method of identifying areas of trainee strengths and weaknesses, good teaching is difficult, if not impossible. Instructors' reluctance may stem from a feeling that tests are too academic for use in a business or industrial training activity. In addition, some instructors may lack confidence in their ability to construct defensible—that is, *valid*—measurement items.

With these assumptions in mind, I have included in this text some suggestions for:

- the need for testing
- the construction of different types of tests
- the criteria of good test items
- the use of tests
- steps in good test administration

Therefore, the major purpose of *Test Construction for Training Evaluation* is to show instructors (and others) in business and industry how they can best construct and use test items. The practical applications of test items have thus been emphasized rather than abstract measurement theory.

Test Construction could not have been written without the input of many people. I wish to thank those who have brought me to my present appreciation of testing and evaluation. A very special thanks is due all those individuals who have:

- written ambiguous test questions
- included test items on material not covered in the text, classroom, or outside readings
- not allowed enough time for completion of the examination
- presented test questions for which the answer was obvious or gave the answer to one or more other questions

and to many others. I had no difficulty in finding poorly constructed test items to use as examples in this text. Hence, I owe a debt of gratitude to more people than I care to mention here.

I wish to thank all the little people, especially Bashful, Doc, Dopey, Grumpy, Happy, Sleepy, and Sneezy who taught me to whistle while I worked; Tom and Jerry, Bugs Bunny, and Sylvester and Tweety Bird who babysat Charlene, Bruce, and Keith while daddy played author.

I must also mention Hal Elliott because it was his request that caused me to formalize the data contained herein.

Dolores Theresa Crespo Denova deserves a great deal more thanks for her thoughtfulness and courage than it is possible to give here, so I'll do *that* elsewhere.

Charles C. Denova
Redondo Beach, California

Contents

1 Training Evaluation Is a Must

A question often asked is:

Is evaluation necessary?

Evaluation is necessary in order to be able to report on the effectiveness of the training activities. To determine if the best, most economical training activities were conducted, an analysis of every aspect of training is a must. The planning process is not complete without a specific plan for evaluation. An effective evaluation plan covers three major areas.*

Area One: The assessment of the change in behavior by those individuals exposed to the training situation or activities.

Area Two: An analysis of whether or not the training activities further the attainment of the goals and objectives of the business enterprise.

Area Three: An evaluation of the training personnel, methods, and materials.

*Denova, Charles C. *Establishing A Training Function: A Guide for Management.* Englewood Cliffs, N.J.: Educational Technology Publications, 1971.

A follow-up of the participants is a must to determine how effective each is using their training on the job. In addition, the follow-up serves as a means of improving future instruction and, generally, uncovers any need for remedial training. Management uses the evaluation information to insure that the intentions are actually realized and that the desired effects are achieved.

DEVELOPING AN EVALUATION PLAN

Training activities are improved most efficiently and intelligently if a continuous appraisal is made of the current situation and of the possible worthwhile changes. Training departments cannot escape making value judgments about their services. The only question to be decided by the training administrator is whether the evaluation is to be conscious and systematic, or instinctive and disorganized. (And who will admit to performing in a disorganized manner?)

When the evaluation is systematic, it is more defensible. The evaluation program must measure a broad range of objectives by a variety of techniques. The evaluation plan must integrate the results into an understanding of the situation that will permit changes that will result in better training programs. On the other hand, an evaluation plan that is haphazard or disorganized may lead to changes that have little or no relationship to the real needs of the business enterprise.

The first consideration must be to determine the purpose for which training activities are evaluated. One of the major purposes of evaluation is to determine the effectiveness of the program. Every training activity, course, or program fulfills a specific purpose. An evaluation plan enables the training administrator to make sound judgments regarding the extent to which the purposes are being met.

Many times, a decision to establish a training course is made on an *educated guess* or a hunch. Generally, the best guesses are made under the pressure of a situation. Therefore, another good reason for evaluation is to validate and clarify any guessing. Stated another way, evaluation proves or disproves the training staff's hypotheses. Assumptions are frequently made regarding the nature of the trainees as well as the total curriculum content. A third reason for conducting evaluation is to answer the question: *Are we offering the experiences most needed by our employees?*

Oftentimes, instructors and training administrators conduct programs without checking to see if desirable outcomes result from their instructional activities. Evaluation helps provide data by which the training staff can be more certain of the extent of progress. It is most important to determine whether the training program is *really* making any difference in the behavior of employees. In addition, it is important to investigate the impact of the training program on the profit picture of the total business enterprise.

Important: The *only* reason for conducting a training program is an economic one.

Finally, a further purpose of evaluation lies in the responsibility of the training administrator to determine how well the training department staff is performing. Therefore, the purposes of evaluating training activities are:

1. to check on the effectiveness of the program.
2. to validate assumptions on which the department is operating.
3. to provide information for curriculum revision.
4. to improve job performance of the training staff by appraising the results of their efforts.
5. to offer data to top management that they have built a sound staff that provides reality training activities in order for the employee to do a most effective job.

Most people engaged in employee developmental work will give at least lip service to the purpose of training and development activities. Before an adequate evaluation can be attempted, however, there must be an understanding and agreement on what the objectives are of the activities to be evaluated. This agreement is of prime importance because the sequence to be followed in an evaluation plan involves:

Step 1. Determination of the Objectives of the Training Activity.
Step 2. A Statement Beforehand of the Criteria that Will Be Accepted as Evidence that the Stated Objectives Are Being Met.
Step 3. Investigation for the Presence and the Extent of the Criteria Stated in Step 2.
Step 4. Writing Out of the Test Items or Process to Determine if the Objectives Have Been Met.

Determining Objectives. Clarifying objectives involves careful consideration. Stating objectives is a difficult and time-consuming task. Yet, without determining and clarifying objectives for the training activity, valid evaluation is not possible. The training objectives must include these basic goals:

1. basic knowledge required
2. basic skill to be acquired
3. economic efficiency
4. staff effectiveness

The process of hammering out statements of objectives of specific training activities is very likely to be a significant experience for all who are involved. The process is not difficult, but it is time-consuming.

Criteria for Evaluation. After many statements of objectives are written, criteria must be established to be used as evidence relating to those objectives. Whatever the criteria are to be, they *must* be defined in measureable terms.

A fundamental measure of learning is a must. Since learning consists of changing behavior, the amount of change must be determined. The training staff that is formulating measurable criteria related to the program objectives needs to investigate previously known and/or previously missing knowledge of skills. The changes (hopefully, gains) can then be attributed to the training program.

Measurement. Once the criteria for evaluation have been set, a way must be found to measure the established criteria. The next step involves the task of applying the measurement technique decided upon. It is worthwhile not to tell the training staff where they have been, but to point out what they must do to arrive at their stated objective.

AN ADEQUATE EVALUATION PLAN

An adequate evaluation plan should have these characteristics:

1. The evaluation plan for each training program must be part of the program planning, and the evaluation program must be comprehensive.
2. The training staff must not ignore program areas while waiting for the "testmakers" to design a precision instrument for measurement. If the training area is important enough to be included, it is important enough to be measured. The training staff must develop a method of measuring all areas covered in the training program.
3. The evaluation must focus on changes in a trainee's behavior. A meaningful evaluation plan cannot be developed unless desired behavior changes relevant to company objectives are stated prior to training.
4. The evaluation program must be continuous. It cannot be an end-of-the-year process. If its purpose is to improve training activities and if its instructional activities are continuous, then the evaluation plan is an ongoing process.
5. Evaluation must be related to curriculum development. The training activities can be evaluated, and changes deemed necessary as the result of the evaluation program can be made.
6. The evaluation should involve the widest possible participation of company personnel. Too frequently, training evaluation programs involve only members of the training staff. However, the people who ultimately must use the products of the training activities—the supervisory staff—should be involved. What better group is there to conduct

the follow-up evaluation after the trainees are at their work station than their immediate supervisors?*

MEASURING INSTRUCTIONAL OUTCOMES

Since skills and knowledge are the most tangible instructional and learning outcomes, they can be measured by various types of tests. Woodruff lists ten instructional and learning outcomes:**

1. Skills.
2. Knowledge.
3. Concepts.
4. Understandings.
5. Applications.
6. Activities.
7. Appreciation.
8. Attitudes.
9. Interests.
10. Adjustments.

How do you determine what are the important things in an evaluation situation? Much of the assessment process rests on *values*, such as:

- Values of the instructor.
- Values of/to the trainees' department.
- Values of the company.
- Values of the occupation or information area in general.

Tangible Outcomes

There are two types of instructional outcomes that are considered highly tangible—*skills and knowledge.* An instructor can readily design a test to determine whether or not individuals possess certain skills and that can specify with reasonable accuracy the degree of skill possessed. In addition, the instructor can test the knowledge possessed or not possessed by individuals and the level of knowledge evidenced in specific content areas.

*Denova, Charles C. Training evaluation causes change in behavior. *Personnel Administration,* September 1969.
**Woodruff, Asahel D. *The Psychology of Teaching.* New York: Logmans, Green and Co., 1951.

Intangible Outcomes

Intangible outcomes include such things as concepts, understandings, applications, appreciations, attitudes, interests, and adjustments. These types of outcomes are more complex than skills and knowledge. Therefore, their measurement is more difficult.

WHY TEST?

Some training personnel have criticized tests as being too academic for use in business and industrial training activities. These critics argue that employees resent or are at least suspicious of being asked to take tests. There is some truth in their arguments. The resentments workers have toward tests can often be curbed if they realize that the information gathered by the testing is needed as an aid to the instructor. Tests are useful only if they help in making decisions, decisions about a trainee, about a method of instruction, about a curriculum, and about the instructor.

Tests have their weaknesses. It is safe to say that tests usually work better than subjective judgments. What would instructors use if tests were not available? On what would they base decisions? They would base decisions solely on observation. The difficulty with this is that it favors the outgoing, glib, self-confident individual to the detriment of the less confident, shy, but often more knowledgeable person. In addition, observations would probably be done on the basis of only a few hours of experience with the trainee. Like any other observer, instructors are prey to typical errors. They have their own idiosyncratic definitions of what constitutes superior abilities—ones that would not necessarily be shared by others in the same situation.

Without tests, how could instructors judge the effectivenss of the methods of instruction? Instructional effectivity decisions might be influenced by things which are unrelated to the issue. The purpose of tests is to help take the personal element and guess work out of decisions. Tests have their weaknesses, but they usually are far more effective than the alternative means in meeting most objectives of evaluation. Because there is nothing better to employ, it is not sensible to discuss whether or not tests *should* be used. Rather, the important points to discuss are *how* tests should be used and what procedures can be employed to make tests more effective.

Tests can be used in the following manner to:

- Locate strengths and/or weaknesses.
- Indicate which topics need to be discussed.
- Determine which topics are already understood.
- Measure change.
- Evaluate the effectiveness of instruction.
- Act as a stimulus to learning new review materials covered.

- Measure the individual abilities of the learners.
- Stimulate discussion and channel thinking.
- Find the knowledge level of the group.
- Determine how well the instructor is teaching (covering the topics determined to be important).
- Measure how well participants are progressing in the learning environment.
- Determine how well the training experience predicted on-the-job performance.

The construction, administration, and scoring of tests are among the most difficult and time-consuming chores of teaching. Many instructors who otherwise do excellent teaching jobs fail when it comes to preparing and using tests. If tests hold difficulties for instructors and are unpleasant to trainees, why use them? Tests are used because they supply some very important information that would be difficult, if not impossible, to obtain by any other means.

THE VALUE OF TESTS TO THE INSTRUCTOR

Tests have value to the instructor primarily in determining the extent to which trainees are meeting the objectives of a unit of instruction. Such objectives should be explicitly stated. Both the instructor and trainees live by these objectives. Only to the extent that the average trainee meets them can the instructor feel satisfaction with the instruction as a whole and the progress of each individual trainee. Tests are very helpful because they supply one of the most important sources of information as to how well both instructors and trainees are meeting the objectives of a unit of instruction.

In order to provide information that helps in decision making, it is necessary that the test represent a comprehensive sample of the important material in the lesson. If the test is slanted toward a particular aspect of the subject matter, to the detriment of other important areas then the test provides a poor base for making decisions. If the test concerns only trivial aspects of the subject matter, rather than the more important ones, decisions based upon such test items can be faulty. Tests provide instructors with clues about the value of what is actually taught, and what is emphasized. When instructors look carefully at the content of their tests, they can see what subject matter they consider important. Many instructors do not realize what values they have with respect to various aspects of their specialties until they see what they place value on in their tests.

How does the instructor know when the learning has succeeded in achieving the specified objectives? (It must be remembered that the primary interest is in determining when and what the learners will be doing when they are demonstrating their grasp of the stressed material.) The answer is to prepare the test items immediately after specifying the objectives. The preparation of the test items at this point can prevent developing a test that measures incidental material in the lesson session rather than how well the specific objectives were achieved.

Test results provide instructors with indications of what was taught and how well the subject was covered. If some trainees do much better on some types of questions in a test than others, it is an indication of how well they were instructed in the subject matter. The value of teaching methods and instructional materials are unknown until their effects are measured.

One of the most fundamental mistakes made by business and industrial trainers is to pitch the level of training sessions too high or too low. In most cases, the trainer assumes what the existing level of knowledge or skill is. Tests can give some indication of what level each individual is at. This information can be used to sell the need for training as well as point out areas for specific emphasis in the instruction.

Workers seek to improve themselves by learning new skills and techniques in their occupations. If they are required to begin their learning process at a level of work they believe they are already competent in, they will be uninterested in being trained. Similarly, if they are assigned work beyond their abilities, they will become discouraged and lose interest.

The value of tests to the instructor may be summarized as follows:

1. Tests indicate to the instructor whether or not the presentation of the subject is sufficiently effective to accomplish the stated objectives. Therefore, the tests should be designed to discover whether the trainees have acquired the desired attitudes, knowledges or abilities. Since the *instructor's* primary objective is to prepare employees to do company-related jobs, job proficiency is the desired end result.

2. Tests highlight those points the instructor did not make clear. The instructor should then review and clarify these points. In this manner, tests assist in developing understanding during the explanation phases of instruction. It is important that tests serve as diagnostic tools for both the instructor and the trainees.

3. Tests enable the instructor to compare the effectiveness of different teaching techniques.

4. Tests identify those trainees who are experiencing difficulty with the subject. The instructor can then give personal attention and guidance to specific trainees, pointing out what they are doing right and what they are doing wrong, and making suggestions for improvement. For maximum learning, trainees must be aware of their own progress. Tests allow the trainees to know how they are doing.

5. Tests can be used to determine whether the trainees have achieved a level of competency to satisfy the certification or promotional standards of the company. Quality of performance is relative, and all jobs will have an established set of objective standards. If there are no

standards, the instructor should develop a set and have them checked for reasonableness and appropriateness.

Caution: To set an impossible standard in order to wash out a large number of trainees is just as bad as setting a standard so low that incompetent trainees are given the training department's stamp of approval.

Tests can be used to discover the particular elements of the training activities in which the participants may be weak. By using tests, the instructor can discover why learning has not resulted from the training activity. The instructor is obligated to permit the trainee to understand why the learning is incomplete if the difficulty is to be overcome. In other words, if the lesson content was important enough to be measured by a test and if the trainee failed to demonstrate mastery, then that element of the lesson must be made clear to the learner.

Note: If it is important enough to test for, then it must be important that everyone understands it.

THE VALUE OF TESTS TO TRAINEES

In addition to the information supplied to instructors, tests also supply valuable information to trainees. Trainees often are unsure about how well they are doing in a unit of instruction. Trainees who do poorly on tests are warned to work harder, work differently, or seek help. During long periods of instruction, tests also provide the trainees with information about what the instructor values and intends to stress in the unit of instruction. Tests can also be used to indicate which topics need to be discussed and which topics are already understood. In this vein, tests have been known to motivate the shy and less confident to participate more in discussions and/or training activities.

Tests have value to the participants in training activities for the following reasons:

1. Test performance indicates to the trainee what progress is being made. Tests measure achievement. Trainees can compare their accomplishment with that of others, as well as with their own previous work.
2. Tests identify those parts of the training activities in which the participant is weak. Tests assist in the diagnosis of areas of difficulty.
3. Tests influence trainees to review the work covered. This helps them organize and retain knowledge.
4. Tests (especially the performance types) give the trainee an oppor-

tunity to practice the application of fundamental principles to various problem situations.

5. Tests assist the participants in distinguishing between the relevant and the irrelevant. (This is an important use of tests and rests squarely on shoulders of the instructor and/or the test designer.)

6. Tests can give incentive and can stimulate the laggard trainee to make a greater effort.

7. Tests are a measure of attainable objectives. Therefore, tests give the trainee a better conception of the objectives of the training activity. In addition, tests may afford an insight to company objectives.

Tests can be very helpful in assisting learners to improve their skills and understanding. Tests must be prepared and administered with the idea in mind that they are effective teaching devices. In order to accomplish this purpose, the instructor must review tests thoroughly after they have been scored and returned to the trainees. It is important that this review be done as soon as possible after administration of the test in order that incorrect thinking by the testees may be corrected as early as possible.

> *Note:* Measurement is essential to the individual's progressive learning capacity.

THE VALUE OF TESTS TO MANAGEMENT

Tests have value to managers because they assist in preparing reports on the effectiveness of training activities. The personnel responsible for training programs must never lose sight of the fact that the primary objective of training is to develop better qualified employees. All too often in the search for the best training, training administrators in their evaluation technique stress whether the participants *enjoyed* the course or program. This emphasis should be shifted to whether the training program produced a better qualified employee. Top management cares most about evaluations that show how much better the employees do on the job as a result of the training they received.

> *Important:* If a trainee's abilities and capabilities are not measurable, a knowledge of the individual is . . . impossible.

The organization responsible for training activities must establish a reputation for employing and maintaining a highly qualified instructional staff. Evaluation of training personnel, their methods and techniques and the instructional materials used, is an ongoing process. The evaluation and testing process must be designed to fit into the total program. This process should start at the same time training activities are planned. Analysis of plans for the evaluation of training activities in business and industry is not simple, nor is it easy if the job is to be done thoroughly. But evaluation must be done.

EXAMINATION VS. EVALUATION

As a phase of the instructional process, examination comes after application. Examination for the purpose of evaluating what learning is taking place is a continuous process. In fact, trainee performance valuation must be integrated into every other aspect of the offered training and development activities. As manager of the learning environment, the instructor provides questions during the presentation and/or application phases of instructional activities to spot check trainee progress.

Tests should be presented as a means of assisting trainees to evaluate their own work and progress. The instructor must tie in trainee evaluation with motivation so that trainees can recognize when they are getting somewhere. It is most important that each trainee has a sense of achievement.

SUMMARY

The evaluation of training is not a necessity . . . *it is a must*! Evaluation is necessary in order to determine:

- If the developmental objectives were achieved.
- The effectiveness of the methods of instruction.
- If the best, most economical training activities were conducted.
- The effectiveness of the methods of instruction.
- Trainee changes of behavior.

Many tests have been criticized as being too academic for use in business and industrial training activivities. While some tests have their weaknesses, it can be said that testing works better than subjective judgment on decisions regarding the value of training. Tests are of value to the:

1. *Instructor,* because they supply one of the most important sources of information as to how well the instructor (as well as the trainee) is meeting the objectives of the unit of instruction.
2. *Trainee* since they indicate what progress the trainee is making, assists in the diagnosis of the areas of difficulty, helps distinguish between the relevant and the irrelevant, and can provide incentives toward greater effort.
3. *Training management* who uses tests to assist in the assessment of the instructional personnel, teaching methods and materials, and whether

or not the training activities do further the attainment of the goals and objectives of the business.

4. *Top management* because of the value test results are in preparing reports on the effectiveness of the entire training and development operation.

An evaluation and testing process must be designed into the training programs and activities in the initial planning phase. Evaluation is not simple, nor is it easy. Yet it must not be overlooked.

2   Principles of Test Construction

Too much emphasis cannot be placed on a realistic outlook on test construction. A point made many times in this book is economy in test construction, administration, and interpretation. Our major purpose is to show instructors how they can best exert themselves in the construction and use of tests. A direct relationship exists between the amount of time and effort one can expect to spend in the formulation of objectives of instruction and the construction of tests to measure progress of individuals with respect to those objectives.

A lot of time must be spent on outlining specific objectives, checking the objectives against the subject matter to be taught, and transforming those objectives into an efficient examination. Although instructors should do the best that they can with the time they have available, it is unreasonable to expect each test to be a paragon of measurement. Doing so is a waste of company money.

Good tests do not arise from sudden inspiration or last-minute desperation. Good test items are planned in advance. The first step in planning a test is to outline the objectives of a unit of instruction. Although instructors do not usually have much time to lavish on the planning of tests, they can at least jot down the major areas of content to be covered by some type of measurement. The amount of time spent in constructing an outline during the planning phase is repaid by the relative speed with which test items can be constructed once the outline is available as a guide. In addition to promoting representativeness for the tests, an outline also provides the instructor with insights about what is to be taught. After looking at test item outlines, it is often easy for instructors to see that they either are not emphasizing important material in their instruction or are including inappropriate items in their tests.

ORGANIZATION OF INSTRUCTION

Good presentation of a lesson does not just happen; it is very carefully planned. Systematic analysis provides the instructor with the structural framework for course development. During analysis, the instructor selects those tasks to be presented, identifies all the instructional materials to be used, decides upon the teaching methods by which the information will be presented, and selects the manner in which the specific objectives will be measured. The following four steps are important to the organization of instructional activities.

Step 1. Identifying the Program

What to teach plagues everyone in a training situation. Normally, subject matter is selected and taught in order to develop knowledge, skills, and/or attitudes.

Step 2. Defining the Trainee Population

Once the subject matter area has been identified, it is a good idea to write a description of the learners for whom the training is intended. Writing it out is necessary to aid in the decision-making that occurs during the organization of instructional material. Whatever their shortcomings and limitations are, it seems reasonable to start where they are.

> *Note:* No matter what arguments are advanced to the contrary, the fact remains that the individuals chosen for a particular class are the ones to be trained.

Step 3. Specifying the Objectives

The importance of preparing statements of objectives for each educational and/or training intent cannot be over-emphasized. To be effective, the statements must specify what the learners will be doing when they are demonstrating that they have achieved the training objectives. A good outline of objectives for a unit of instruction helps guide the instructor toward the

THE SEQUENCE OF TRAINING ACTIVITIES

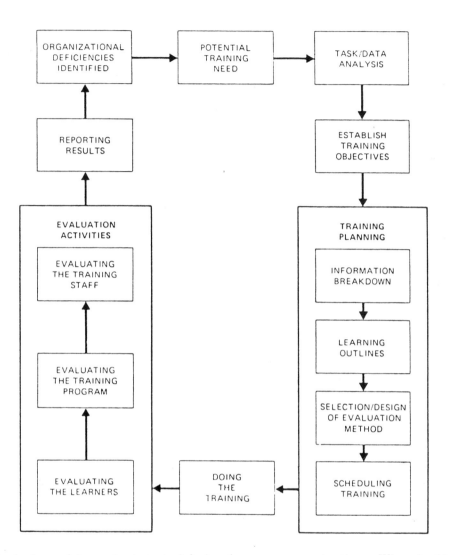

inclusion of important materials in classroom examinations. When looking at an outline of objectives, the instructor is encouraged to stress items regarding relatively high levels of understanding rather than those that concern only simple details.

Step 4. Specifying Terminal Knowledge

How does instructor know when the learner has succeeded in achieving the specified objectives? Prepare a series of test items that will indicate what the learner has accomplished.

Important: The preparation of the examination at this point is to prevent the instructor from writing a test that measures *merely what happens* to be included in the lesson rather than a test that measures *how well* the specified objectives were achieved.

STEPS IN TEST CONSTRUCTION

One of the important steps in the learning process is the periodic measurement of progress and the evaluation of the results of a training program. In technical training, for example, this is done by written tests, performance tests, and observance of practical exercise being accomplished by the trainee. Most training is evaluated by performance or the development of skills, but written tests have their place and are given for the following reasons:

- To measure the trainee's achievement and understanding.
- To discover weakness in instruction.
- To diagnose trainee difficulties.
- To determine level of performance.
- To give the trainee incentive.

Test construction is the writing of examination items and exercises designed to measure the degree to which individuals have attained the desired outcome of training activities. The following are major steps in test construction.

1. *Determine the scope of the test.* Does the test cover a lesson, a unit, a phase, a specific job, or some other measurable part of the training activities?

2. *Determine what is to be measured.* What was the objective of the training program? Design a test that measures attitudes, abilities, skills, or mastery of principles and/or facts.

3. *Select the test items.* Write items for each topic and/or subtopic without regard for the number of test items that will be used in the final draft. Prepare as many examination items as possible.

4. *Select the technique.* Try to select the testing technique most suitable for the purpose of the test. Always keep in mind the objective of the training program.

5. *Fix the length of the text.* Choose the number of items that will cover the instructional material adequately.

6. *Select the final items.* Choose those items that treat the most essential and significant portions of instruction. Never use a test item to measure material not covered by the instructional activities.

7. *Arrange the items in final form.* Group similar items together and arrange them in an approximate order of their difficulty.

8. *Prepare directions for the test.* The instructor is obligated to make it perfectly clear what the trainee is to do and how the trainee is to do it.

9. *Prepare a scoring device.* Scoring devices aid in the speed and accuracy of evaluating the trainees.

10. *Question the questions:*

a. Does the question cover an important or useful aspect of the training lesson, course, and/or program?
b. Is the question stated in the language of the learner?
c. Does the wording give away the answer?
d. Does this question give the answer to another question?
e. Is the question phrased in the negative? If so, change it.
f. Is this test item just on memory? Items should measure application, not just the memorizing of facts.
g. Is the test item of a catch or leading type? The trick question should be avoided!

Good tests do not happen simply as a product of last-minute inspiration. Good tests are planned in detail well in advance. The testing plan is directly tied in with the objectives of the unit of instruction and the training program in general. It takes patience to construct good tests. Test construction is time-consuming.

The following are the specific points to observe in constructing test items:

1. List all key points covered in the training activities.
2. Determine, with respect to each key point, what is required:
   a. recall,
   b. recognition,
   c. problem-solving, or
   d. skill.
3. Increasing the number of test items tends to increase reliability.
4. Include several types of items on the test.
5. True-false items reduce test reliability.
6. When it is necessary to grade trainees, using a formula that corrects for guessing is not recommended.
7. Keep weighting of items to a minimum. If a point is highly important, include several test items on that point.
8. Include complete directions for each type of test item. Include an example showing how each type of item is to be answered.
9. Word each item in the simplest possible manner.
10. Do not "lift" statements directly from books.
11. Underline key words, but don't overdo it.
12. Avoid "curve-ball" test items, the catch questions, or the "trick" question.
13. Do not include one item that supplies the answer to another.
14. Do not include any item for which the answer is obvious to a person who does not know the subject matter.
15. There should be only one correct and undisputed answer.

16. The choice of answers should deal with similar rather than unrelated ideas.
17. The questions should require the trainee to use knowledge gained rather than to demonstrate memory for small detailed facts.
18. Avoid questions that can be answered solely on the basis of general knowledge not included in the classroom activities.
19. Avoid asking questions on trivial details.
20. Ingenuity in construction of items adds to their interest; also, diagrams, pictures, and graphs help clarify the test items.
21. Keep the language and punctuation clear.
22. State each item in the working language of the trainee.
23. Use plausible choices.
24. Scatter the position of the correct answers. Avoid setting a pattern.
25. Each item should test only one idea.

All tests should be constructed solely from the objectives of the training program. Working from a statement of objectives, you should be able to divide the statement into the level of knowledge or skill to be tested.

For example:

Objective: Given a list of merchandise and its prices, the trainee will be able to prepare sales slips without error.

Level of behavior to be tested: be able to prepare (blank) without error"

Topic area to be tested: sales slips.

Objective: The trainee will be able to state the seven general features of the NC-3000 radar system.

Level of behavior to be tested: be able to state (blank).

Topic area to be tested: seven general features of the NC-3000 radar system.

Working from the statements of objectives, divide each objective into its level of test behavior (generally, the complete verb) and the objective topic area (generally the direct object and modifiers). This is done until all specific objectives have been divided as illustrated. This action provides a test item base list. Prepare as many test items as necessary to determine how well trainees meet each objective.

Important: Create items that call for the same kind of behavior as that specified in the objectives.

The level of test behavior is stated in the objectives. In addition, the type of test item to be constructed is influenced by the objectives. For example:

1. Use essay or completion questions when the level of behavior is to:

   - Describe.
   - State.
   - Define.
   - Determine.
   - Calculate.
   - Specify.
   - Label.
   - List.

2. Use multiple-choice or matching questions when the level of behavior is to:

   - Select.
   - Identify.
   - Recognize.
   - Indicate.
   - Differentiate.
   - Describe.
   - Match.
   - Calculate.

   Important: The test sequence should always follow the order in which the behaviors are to be performed on the job.

The skill of developing tests, especially written ones, involves two interrelated components: first, the technical information that has an effect on the different test items, and second, a test of the author's journalistic skill.

PRETEST/POST-TEST

A pretest can be used to determine the trainees' level of skills and/or knowledge as specified in the objectives. Pretests can determine whether the group scheduled for training already know the material in the program or whether they possess the prerequisite skill and/or knowledge required to take part in the program. Most important, a pretest can form the basis for a post-test comparison. A post-test can be given to determine:

1. How well the end-of-training performance of the participants coincides with the stated objectives.
2. Which objectives were not accomplished.
3. Program/course effectiveness.
4. The amount the participants learned.
5. The effectiveness of the instructor, the instructional materials, and the teaching techniques.

TYPES OF TESTS

In this book, ideas for the construction of instructional test items are divided into essay and objective tests.

Essay Tests (Subjective)

In an essay examination, the testees are given a few questions to which they respond in some detail. The results of essay examinations tend to be subjective, in that much of the instructor's evaluation is based on personal judgment rather than on objective features that can be listed. Do essay questions provide an opportunity for learners to show how well they can organize their thoughts? Yes, if the test is well constructed.

Long-answer essay questions give a distinct advantage to individuals who write well (even if they do not know a great deal about the subject matter). The worst fault of the long-answer essay question is unreliability of scoring. Therefore, several short answer questions are by far a better method of testing.

Objective Tests

In an objective test, the scoring procedure can be completely stated before the administration of the test—it can be graded/scored *objectively*. In addition, the instructor's errors in personal judgment are eliminated. The rules for scoring are absolutely clear: the answer to each test item is either right or wrong regardless of who scores the test. Every examination, then, must have clearly stated instructions on how to *take* the test. Objective tests have the following advantages:

- Generally, it does not take much time for the trainee to answer the test items.
- They are easy to score/grade. Sometimes this can be done by a machine.
- In a given amount of time, they can cover a greater scope of the instructional material than can any other test method.

Objective tests are often criticized because they:

- are basically knowledge tests and so do not measure the trainee's ability to apply methods of analysis.
- measure only the memory of simple facts and trivial details.
- provide no opportunity to determine how well individuals can organize their thoughts.
- measure none of the learner's critical or creative abilities.
- do not give the trainees any opportunity to express themselves in writing.

Important: The prime disadvantage of objective tests is that valid ones are extremely difficult to construct.

Objective vs. Essay

There are no set rules to follow in determining when to use essay test items instead of objective test items. The decision whether to use objective or essay test items depends on:

- The number of participants to be tested.
- The specific subject matter.
- The preferences of the instructor.
- The test construction skills of the instructor.
- The background and experience of the participants.

There are also three other categories of tests:

Oral: Used in each training session as a spot check of trainee progress.

Written: Used to cover large areas of instruction and to measure knowledge acquired.

Performance: Used to measure the learner's ability to do or perform a given task (mental or physical).

DEVELOPING GOOD TEST ITEMS

Writing effective test items is one of the instructor's most difficult tasks. Not only is the actual writing of test items difficult, the following factors also play an important part:

1. Item construction requires considerable time and effort, demanding mastery of the subject matter.
2. The writer must possess the skill to visualize joblike situations for use in developing problems and have an ability to write clearly.
3. The instructor must be aware of the relative value of items and be able to arrange questions in random order as well as in order of difficulty.
4. Items must be created that pinpoint small differences between levels of achievement of trainees.
5. The instructor is required to understand the individuals for whom the test is intended and understand how the specific objectives of the training can be evaluated. The possible effect factors such as physical facilities, temperature, humidity, lighting, time allowed, and time of day have on test realiability must be considered.
6. A knowledge of the various techniques of test item writing is required

that includes an understanding of the function oral and/or written instructions preceding a test have.

The writing of good test items is a difficult, creative task. It is important for the creator of test items to remember that, in themselves, rules do not guarantee good test items. A technically correct item and a grammatically correct item may not include an important idea for measuring anything worthwhile.

Regardless of the test item type, and to increase the chances of success in writing good test items, the following principles of construction should be followed:

1. Each item must test a concept that is important for the trainee to know, understand, and be able to apply.
2. Each item must be stated so that most people with competence in the subject matter will agree on the correct response.
3. Each item must be stated in the language of the subject matter objectives being tested.
4. The wording of each item must be simple, direct, and free of ambiguity.
5. Sketches, diagrams, pictures, tables, and all other necessary items must be included when they are necessary for the trainee to visualize the problem well.
6. As a whole, the test items must present a situation that demands knowledge of the job or the subject matter.
7. No item should reveal the correct response to another item.

Important: Good test items do not simply happen as a product of last minute inspiration. They must be planned in detail well in advance.

THE WORDING OF GOOD TEST ITEMS

Words are the basic tool in writing test items. They have meaning, purpose, and power. It is important to use simple, concrete words in preference to complex or abstract ones. There is no learning principle or testing and measurement law that requires big words be used. There are lots of small words that can be made to say what you want to. There are many small words that work as well as the big ones, frequently even better. Simple, short words communicate immediately. Small words work well because we all know what they mean. They stimulate sense memory. They enable the learner to identify immediately what is being measured.

Small words are usually to the point, can be rich with the right feeling or thought, and can be made to say what it is you want to the way it should be said. Long, complex words take longer for comprehension. Many learners cannot readily see, feel, or grasp longer, more abstract words. Abstract words tend to be too vague to be used effectively in test construction. In addition, small words are easy to move. Big words are heavy; become bogged down. Worse yet, many times, big words get in the way of what it is that must be said.

The right word in the right place is more important than whether the word is small or large, concrete or abstract. The right word is the one that expresses the desired meaning and achieves the purpose or objective. When the chosen word is unfamiliar to the trainee, it fails to communicate.

> *Important Credo:* I will use simple words; I will explain unfamiliar terms.

FIT THE TESTS INTO THE INSTRUCTIONAL PATTERN

As stated before, good lessons do not just happen; they must be carefully planned. The proper times when the instructor should administer tests must be planned in advance also. The instructor must integrate evaluation into each aspect of the teaching-learning cycle, orienting test items to clearly define course objectives. Testing must be geared to the skills and applications of information needed by the trainee for on-the-job performance.

> *Note:* An instructor cannot evaluate trainee behavior without considering what the on-the-job behavior should be.

Classroom motivation incentives must be integrated with the evaluation of trainee performance. Trainees must be rewarded for their efforts; they must experience the satisfaction that accompanies success. In addition to feeling that they can do the job, trainees must be encouraged to be aware of their progress. They must know which of their efforts is right and have weaknesses detected and corrected. Therefore, diagnostic testing and evaluation for remedial and motivational purposes is an integral part of the instructional process.

> *Note:* Testing is important to learning and should not be separated from instruction.

Examine carefully the course objectives. Choose objectives that result in action. Select skills that trainees can relate to the job. Construct problem situations and test items that are realistic in terms of the job. Evaluation of job proficiency is more important than evaluation or grasp of the training course subject content.

SUMMARY

A test is a measuring instrument. The designer of a measuring device must know what can be measured as well as what is to be measured. Achievement tests can be used to measure the ability of the trainee to recall ideas, recognize correct responses in an appropriate situation, and apply principles to the solution of problems. They can be used to measure skills.

Achievement tests are frequently given for the purpose of grading trainees. Tests should be given frequently in order to discover gaps in learning, so that any must-know ideas or skills can be reviewed, and future instruction can be improved.

After the test has been constructed, the following questions should be answered.

1. Does the wording give away the answer?
2. Do the questions cover important or useful aspects of the course?
3. Are the questions stated in the language of the trainee?
4. Does one question give the answer to another one?
5. When a negative word or phase is used, is it underlined for emphasis?
6. Are the questions just tests of memory? (Test for application, not merely memory.)
7. Are any of the items catch or leading questions? (They should be avoided).

Any good test is valid, reliable, and mechanically simple. If tests are to be used for grading trainees, they must also be discriminating, comprehensive, as objective as possible, and cover a range of difficulty. The most important test characteristic is validity.

3   Essay Test Items

Essay test items work effectively when the instructional methods stress a *Gestält* concept (wholeness). Essay questions should be used to measure objectives dealing with understanding, attitudes, interests, creativity, and verbal expression. Creativity and original thinking are poorly stimulated or measured by choice-type items. Freedom of response is the invaluable strength of the essay test items, whose major strengths are:

1. Freedom of expression and creativity.
2. Emphasis on a participant's depth and scope of knowledge of the subject matter.

Essay tests should be used for subjects for which these objectives are important. It would be difficult to evaluate the effect of a report-writing course and measure its accomplishments without essay test items. There is also a weakness inherent in essay testing by instructors in the lack of planning the possible use and construction of the essay test. It is not uncommon for an instructor to walk into a classroom and write one broad, ambiguous essay question on the chalkboard.

Note: Good tests don't just happen. They are planned.

The planning of essay test items must take into account the following:

- The limited nature of the test sample.
- The time limits of the training activities.
- The choice of subject matter adaptable to the test sample.
- The major objective of the training activity.

One of the most overlooked items in test planning and construction is the basis and/or method to be used for grading and scoring the answers, which is very critical. The following are some of the questions the test designer should ask of each essay test:

1. Are the objectives to be measured adaptable to essay test items?
2. Do the test takers have sufficient background to respond to the essay test items?
3. Does the essay test item permit freedom of response to bring out the depth and scope of the test takers' knowledge of the subject matter presented?
4. Has sufficient time been allotted for test takers to plan responses?
5. Are the essay items relevant to the business or are they hypothetical?

Important: Test items relevant to company business is the name of the game.

HINTS ON ESSAY TEST CONSTRUCTION

When responding to essay items, the test takers supply their own answers to each item in their own way. Well-constructed essay questions can be used to measure the learners' ability to deal with subject matter at their level of understanding, to organize their thoughts, and to express themselves in writing. To help ensure that these important aspects of learning are actually measured, several factors should be heeded.

1. Design a relatively large number of test items that require short answers rather than a smaller number of items requiring long answers.

Long-answer questions are prone to a number of faults. Learners often get quite lost in their own answers, tend to repeat themselves, and are not sure when they have said enough. Instructors get lost in reading page after page of responses to one question, forget what the individual said earlier, and have difficulty in forming a reliable impression of the quality of the response.

Another disadvantage of long-answer items is that only a small number of items can be used in the test because of the limited amount of time available for most training examinations in business and industry. This time limit usually results in a poor sampling of the total subject matter to be covered by the test; consequently, chance (measurement error) plays a large part in the results.

Far better than using a relatively small number of long-answer questions is the use of a larger number of short-answer questions. The advantages of well-constructed short-answer questions are:

a. Trainees are more easily aimed at the correct response.
b. Speed of writing is not a strong influence.
c. Instructors have more concrete standards for scoring.
d. The questions can range broadly over the subject matter.

2. Essay questions must be written in the language of the participants and should be precise in meaning and unambiguous and enough detail must be provided in the question to channel the trainees toward the correct response.

One of the major faults of many essay items is that they pose such global or ambiguous questions that even an expert in the field could not provide the instructor with an appropriate answer. The accurate aiming of essay questions is a major part of the art and skill of test construction.

Poor:

What happened to vestibule training during World War II?—This question is so vague and open-ended that almost any answer could follow. In fact, one might write a book on the topic of vestibule training during World War II.

Improved:

Describe the changes in on-the-job training during World War II considering: (a) time factors, (b) manpower build-ups, (c) development of training aids, and (d) sources of federal government support.

Poor:

What are Newton's laws of motion?—This question lacks the needed amount of specification to aim the individuals accurately toward the correct response. Although the instructor included the question on the test for the purpose of finding out whether participants understand Newton's laws of motion, the question, as presently phrased, asks only for a listing of the laws of motion.

Improved:

Describe each of Newton's three laws of motion. Illustrate each with the action of astronauts on the moon.—The major reason why so many essay items fail to aim trainees accurately is that instructors do not supply the specifics of what is meant or desired by the question. In constructing essay items, it takes only a few more minutes to supply the detailed specifications.

Poor:

Evaluate Maslow's hierarchy of needs.

Improved:

Do you agree with Maslow's hierarchy of needs? Compare it to your observations of the people in your organization. Cite any examples of people you feel do not conform to this hierarchy.

Poor:

Discuss Herzberg's motivation-hygiene theory.

Improved:

Using Herzberg's motivation-hygiene theory as the model, describe:
a. How effective you believe wage incentives are as motivators of greater productivity.
b. What effect piece-rate pay has on a worker's output.
A good rule of thumb to use in writing essay questions is to phrase them so that a person who is knowledgeable about the topic but who is not a member of the class would be able to answer them accurately.

3. All individuals must be required to answer the same questions. There should be no optional essay items on the test. Unless all learners answer the same questions, the test is not really standardized. It is difficult to make accurate comparisons between learners when this suggestion is violated and trainees are given, for example, of eight questions to choose any four. Some instructors argue for the use of this procedure because they say it allows trainees to appear at their best.

The purpose of a test is not to see how well the trainees can do if they are allowed to pick their own questions, but rather to determine how proficient they are when tackling a list of representative questions. When the trainees are permitted to choose from among several essay test items, they may avoid those questions designed to measure important objectives.

4. Do not require too much writing for the time available. More often than not, instructors require much more writing than most trainees can complete in the time available. This is done by giving either a few very long answer questions or too many short-answer questions. When too much writing is required, the test turns into a speed-writing contest. To judge the proper amount of writing required of trainees, instructors should first specify the total amount of page space allowed. This amount of space should then be apportioned among the questions.

Poor:

Discuss the managerial grid.—This essay question requires a long answer. The main concern to the management trainee will be how much of an answer does the instructor want. When will the answer cover the topic stated? Is it the desire of the instructor that the trainee rewrite *The Manage-*

rial Grid by Blake and Mouton* in order to answer the above essay question? The answer is obviously: of course not!

Improved:

(1) Briefly state (in 25 words or less) the value to you of the managerial grid. Or: (2) How does the managerial grid relate to the Maslow and Herzberg theories of motivation?—Now the management trainee should feel comfortable when the answer is long enough to cover the question adequately.

Poor:

Describe the Hawthorne experiments.—The details of the Hawthorne experiments are well documented in *Management and the Worker*** by Roethlisberger and Dickson.

Improved:

Describe the importance of the Hawthorne experiments in relation to your area of supervisory responsibility.

5. Phrase questions in such a way that they encourage the demonstration of relatively high levels of understanding. The special virtue of essay tests is that they can be used to measure the ability to organize material and to deal with the subject matter at a high level of understanding. Whether essay questions do perform this function depends on whether they are phrased in such a way as to actually encourage answers at this level. Essay questions should require the trainee to summarize major developments in the topic, to explore relationships, to explain how principles apply to novel situations, or to compare and contrast.

Poor:

In your opinion, is it possible for management to motivate workers to the highest possible level for the organization?—An individual could answer this question with a simple yes or no, which was not the intent of the instructor. If it were, the question is best not asked.

Improved:

In your opinion, is it possible for management to motivate workers to the highest possible level for the organization? If so, what are the important things for management to do? If not, why not?

Poor:

Compare Theory X and Theory Y, managers.

*Blake, Robert R., and Jane S. Mouton, *The Management Grid*. Houston: Gulf Publishing Co., 1964.
**Roethlisberger, F. J., and W. J. Dickson, *Management and the Worker*. Cambridge, Mass: Harvard University Press, 1939.

Improved:

Cite a situation when a Theory Y manager could operate as a Theory X one would.

Poor:

What is manpower planning? Or: Discuss the nature of manpower planning.

Improved:

Discuss the nature of manpower planning and its significance in operations management.

6. Directions for the test should be written out. More often than not, instructors fail to provide explicit directions and instructions for their tests. Many instructors give test directions verbally before the trainee takes the test. Writing out the instructions is important because it allows the test taker to check back in case doubts arise. The following is an excellent essay item. It illustrates all of the seven construction suggestions given in this section of the book.

Question:

Consider the servo system illustrated below. The purpose of the system is to correct deviations from level flight along the longitudinal or pitch axis of the missile airframe. The letters and numbers identify the following units:

1. Gyroscope	F. Electrical Feedback Signal
2. Summing Network	
3. Servo Module	G. Mechanical Feedback Signal
4. Aerodynamic Control Surfaces	
5. Feedback Potentiometer	M. Servo Motor

Explain the reasons for the actions and interrelationships (if any) of as many of the system parts as you can.

(*Note:* Your answer should be approximately 200 words.)

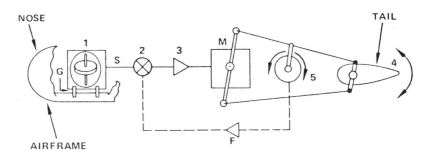

Important: Design essay items that require the trainee to:
Define: Give category.
Compare: State similarities and/or differences.
Contrast: Stress differences.
Explain how: Use logical sequence.
Explain why: Offer reasons.
Illustrate: Provide examples.
Prove: Give evidence.

GRADING ESSAY TESTS

The grading of essay test items is the most time-consuming aspect of using such questions. Careful attention to planning and construction of the essay items can yield time-saving results. Grading standards and an answer key must be established as the essay items are constructed. Construct a grading key that includes the major points the test takers should include in response to each essay test item. Read a single question through on all the papers, assigning the appropriate value to the response on each paper as it is read. Repeat the procedure until all the essay items on all the papers have been read. The advantage of this procedure is that it permits the instructor to evaluate each essay test item through all the papers without changing the mind-set. In addition, this procedure aids in standardizing scoring.

SUMMARY

Essay test items are effective when the training unit stresses the concept of wholeness. The inherent weakness of using essay tests lies in lack of planning during construction of the essay test items. In responding to the essay item, the trainee should be required to make a comparison, write a description, or explain some aspect of the subject matter studied. The essay item becomes useful when it is important to measure the trainee's ability to:

- Organize facts and ideas.
- Reason with or from the knowledge gained.
- Express thoughts and ideas clearly.

The following suggestions should be kept in mind when writing and using essay-type test items:

1. Use essay test items only for those functions for which they are best suited.

2. Design essay items so that they measure the trainee's ability to apply the principles that have been taught.
3. Employ a relatively large number of short-answer items rather than a relatively smaller number of long-answer items.
4. Ask for specific answers.
5. Provide enough detail in the essay question so that the trainee has an outline to follow or is accurately aimed toward the correct formulation of a response.
6. Require all individuals to answer the same questions.
7. All essay items must mean essentially the same thing to everyone who knows the material.
8. Suggest a limit (space, words, and time) for each essay item. (Do not require too much writing for the time available.)
9. Do not use essay items that are linked to the solution of a problem stated or that respond to another question.
10. Phrase essay questions so that they encourage the demonstration of high levels of understanding.

Essay test items have a built-in disadvantage in that their scoring may be influenced by the instructor's level of interest and greater range of knowledge. Another disadvantage is that they take a relatively long time for the trainee to write responses and for the instructor to score or grade them. An essay item also invites the sort of bluffing in which literary skill plays a more important part in answering than a demonstration of trainee's real knowledge of the subject matter.

Important: One of the difficulties in constructing essay items is that the process *appears* to be *so easy.*

4 _____The Oral Question

The oral method of examination is the oldest form of testing. Socrates is often cited as a model in the use of the oral questioning technique. His teaching method was largely a series of leading questions that were open-ended and somewhat forced. They were designed to lead to individual conclusions.

The oral question technique can be used to assess trainee achievement and the effectiveness of an instructor's presentation. When properly planned, constructed, and used, oral questions can serve as a good instructional technique and be valuable as an informal means of appraising the progress of the training activity.

The oral question technique is a most effective teaching devices for developing clear, understandable explanations and for guiding and helping the interaction between instructors and trainees. It is an excellent classroom strategy (although it is sometimes difficult to use). The oral method has a variety of uses in many instructional situations. With it the instructor probably devotes a lot of time and thought to devising and asking questions, becoming a professional question maker. In fact, the instructor who knows how to question skillfully is seldom a poor instructor. By asking questions, an instructor can stimulate thinking and learning. In addition, it is by asking questions and studying the answers to them that an instructor measures and evaluates the thinking and learning process of trainees.

The instructor must make sure that the facts are clearly presented and understood by the trainees. Since clear thinking precedes clear expression, the instructor must allow enough time for learners to digest the question. After the question is asked, the instructor must pause to give the members of the class time to think.

> There must be time to *create*.
> There is always time to *evaluate*.

The instructor can use oral questions in several ways, depending on the purpose.

Purpose:

1. Direct Questioning. One of the most common ways of using oral questions is to direct a question to a particular trainee.

Example: How many degrees are there in a circle, Mr. Smith?—The direct question is used to spot check the effectiveness of instruction, to stimulate trainees' interest and thinking, or to have a trainee contribute experiences; in short, to stimulate participation.

2. The Overhead Question. The overhead question is asked without indicating who is to reply. The question is addressed to the entire class to stimulate thinking and/or discussion.

Example: What is one of the important lessons we learned from the Hawthorne experiments?—A question of this type is usually used to open class discussion, but it may be used any time during the lesson. When an overhead question is used, the instructor should expect several replies and allow everyone who wishes to comment on the question do so.

3. The Relay or Reworded Question. When a trainee asks a question, the instructor may reword the original question slightly or restate it verbatim and pass it on to another trainee for a reply. The use of this method assists the instructor in maintaining a trainee-centered lesson.

> *Caution:* Use the relay question technique only when you are certain that other trainees know the answer. In case of doubt, forget it.

4. The Reverse Question. The reverse question is another method to maintain a trainee-centered lesson. In addition, the reverse question is a teaching technique. When a trainee asks a question, the instructor replies by asking another question that leads the trainee to an answer to the original question. With the use of the reverse or the relay question, the instructor remains

somewhat in the background and, at the same time, promotes (leads, if you will) class discussion.

5. The Rhetorical Question. The rhetorical question is one that is asked merely for effect with no answer expected. With rhetorical questions, the instructor poses the question, pauses momentarily to allow trainees to think about it, then supplies the answer him or herself. This method of questioning is especially effective when introducing new material. Sometimes the rhetorical question may be used to effect an easy transition between points.

QUESTION-AND-ANSWER STANDARDS

The instructor should require trainees to meet certain standards when asking questions and giving answers.

1. A trainee's answer should be heard by everyone in the class. The instructor should tell the trainees to address their questions and answers to the class. A trainee's question must be heard (by repetition, if necessary) before it is answered by the instructor or another trainee.
2. Group answers should be avoided. Trainees should not answer without being called upon.
3. All answers must be recognized according to merit. The instructor must evaluate the answer so that trainees will understand how much value to place on the response. The instructor must give proper credit where it is due. If necessary, for vague answers, have the trainee clarify. (The instructor should clarify only if a trainee cannot). The instructor should avoid repeating answers unless it is absolutely necessary in order that all may hear it.
4. The instructor should encourage trainee success in answers to questions. Do not accept "I don't know" without some attempt to draw a positive response from the trainee.
5. Trainee questions may be answered by other trainees. The instructor should answer a question only when the answer cannot be elicited from other trainees.

TYPES OF ORAL QUESTIONS

Oral examination and evaluation can be divided as follows:

- Those requiring an oral answer—These evaluations are single questions asked of individuals in a classroom situation as instruction progresses. Generally, a single question is posed to each individual. Interview and role-playing techniques are excellent uses of oral questions.
- Those requiring written response—This group of questions can be the

same as the above, except that a single question can be directed to the class as a group.

During training activities, instructors regularly stimulate trainees with these three main types of oral questions:

1. To develop understanding. Remembering is the most common thinking process in a classroom. An instructor may make use of the questioning technique to help the trainees recall essential facts and principles.
2. To prompt reasoning and judgment. Oral questions may be used to stimulate and direct thinking. Well-planned questions can generate the curiosity and interest necessary for thinking and learning. Questions cause trainees to put ideas together into patterns. If the trainee's thinking seems to be far afield, a series of questions can serve to direct thinking back into the appropriate channels. Trainees need to learn ways of deciding whether or not a statement is true, a plan or process is sound, or an action is wisely taken. Questions assist trainees in the development of the capability to reason and judge.
3. As a two-way street. The use of oral questions is a two way proposition. In a well-managed learning environment, questions come from both sides of the classroom, the participants as well as the instructor. The instructor uses them as a teaching method; the trainees ask them because of doubt or curiosity. Questions from learners have a real value; therefore, the instructor is encouraged to develop a classroom atmosphere that stimulates questions and launches creative thinking on the part of trainees. Thinking is the catalyst of learning.

Tips for trainee questions:

- Give consideration to all questions.
- Dispose of trivial questions as courteously as possible.
- Quickly analyze the purpose of the question.
- Give other trainees the first chance at the answer, if it is appropriate to do so.

THE CONSTRUCTION OF ORAL QUESTIONS

The construction of several oral questions is not difficult, but planning is a must. Time must be spent in preparing the questions if the desired measurement objectives are to be accomplished. Questions should be written out ahead of time and must be included in the lesson plan. Acceptable answers should be written out by the instructor for each of the questions developed.

Questions must be selected, worded, and used to accord with the instructor's purposes. Key questions should be written in a sequence that follows the instructor's teaching pattern. The following points should be helpful in planning and constructing key oral questions.

1. Make the wording definite, clear, and concise. Trainees must know and understand exactly what is being asked.
2. Design each question to center on only one idea or concept. Each question must emphasize just one point.
3. Take into consideration individual trainee differences. The question should only be as difficult as the particular stage of training permits, no more or less. A question that is challenging to one trainee may be very easy for a second and unanswerable by a third. Although each question should be adaptable to each trainee's ability level, be sure the questions are all answerable.
4. Phrase the questions to indicate the type of response desired. Each of the following words indicates a specific type of answer:

- Classify.
- Compare.
- Criticize.
- Define.
- Explain.
- Interpret.
- Justify.
- Summarize.
- Verify.

Important: All oral questions must be included in the lesson plan.

ADMINISTERING ORAL QUESTIONS

The skillful administration of oral questions is necessary if good measurement standards are to be achieved. The techniques used in asking questions are as important as constructing them well. The following suggestions may be of value in improving questioning techniques.

1. Distribute the questions asked among all the trainees. This does not mean each trainee is asked exactly the same number of questions; however, avoid calling only on the eager trainees and not involving the timid, quiet ones.

Note: Involve the nonvolunteers. If only one question is asked of each participant, care must be taken to make all questions of comparable difficulty. The instructor can overcome any disparity by constructing several questions per enrollee.

Remember: When only one question is asked of each individual, the oral quiz lacks reliability because the sample is inadequate.

2. Use the *overhead* technique in the following sequences: (1) ask the question, (2) pause, and (3) name a trainee.

This procedure can keep trainees on their toes. Strive to make each trainee consider every question. Address the question to the entire group before calling the name of the one who is to answer. Have the trainee named address the answer to the group. Call on others to evaluate the answer.

> *Important:* Avoid giving the impression that either the questions or the answers are unimportant.

Encourage the trainees to comment on the answers of their classmates. Follow up promising comments and building on the contributions. Do not interrupt the trainee who is attempting to answer or contribute to the question. Wait until five or six of the class members want to speak. Do not drop the trainee too quickly who seems unable to answer; allow time for thought.

3. Keep the repetition of questions to a minimum. Insure audibility, then refuse to repeat questions or answers. Repeating questions encourages inattention and stalling. The instructor should ask questions in a normal conversational tone, loud enough to be heard by all the trainees the first time. The individuals must hear and understand the question if they are to respond successfully. The best method is to read the question loudly, slowly, and with careful enunciation.

4. Do not permit group answers. The attention-grabbing trainees will answer loudly and cover up the quiet or timid ones. This practice can be prevented by calling on the trainees by name.

> *Note:* The instructor must maintain a friendly but businesslike attitude to help establish an informal atmosphere with the program participants.

5. Balance factual and thought-provoking questions to keep the trainees alert. If signs of inattention or daydreaming are detected, a question addressed to the inattentive individuals will arouse them and bring them back into the discussion.

> *Note:* Make sure that the question is designed to get attention rather than to embarrass the individual.

6. Commend good answers. When a trainee answers a question well from the standpoint of current ability, praise the individual for that answer. A little praise always goes a long way.

> *Caution:* Oral questions should never be used to put a trainee

on the spot or to indicate an individual's weakness to the rest of the class.

7. Do not use catch questions. There is no place in a training program for catch questions. An attempt to trick a trainee into making a mistake is not worthy of a good instructor. Catch questions make trainees suspicious of all the questions.

8. Do not use threatening questions. Non-threatening, exploratory questions are very effective for drawing reluctant trainees out and making them think more clearly. Oral questions can also serve to direct attention and discussion to areas that may have been overlooked.

> *Important:* Use oral questions in every training session as a spot check of trainee progress.

Oral questions are more valid than other test forms for measuring training activities in which verbal performance is important. Oral questions are excellent for stimulating the kind of interaction conducive to problem-solving. A set of good oral questions does not just happen. Questions that stimulate and direct thinking must be planned. Key questions to guide trainee development toward definite, specific objectives must be asked. So . . . *Plan to ask them.*

TRAINEE RESPONSE STANDARDS

Instructors should require trainees to meet the following standards when answering oral questions.

1. A trainee's answer should be heard by all of the class. Instructors should tell trainees to address their questions and answers to the class. A trainee's question must be heard (by repetition, if necessary), before it is answered by the instructor or another trainee.
2. Concert or group answers should be avoided, except to provide drill. Trainees should not answer without being called upon.
3. All answers should be recognized according to merit. Evaluate the answer so that trainees will understand how much value to place on the response. Give proper credit where it is due. Elaborate on an answer or have the trainee clarify vague answers. Do not repeat answers unless it is necessary to do so in order that all may hear them.
4. Instructors should encourage trainee success on answers to questions. Do not accept "I don't know" without some attempt to draw a positive response from the trainee.
5. Trainee questions should be answered by other trainees. Instructors

should answer questions only when they cannot elicit answers from other trainees.

SITUATION OR INCIDENT TEST ITEMS

The presentation of various types of questions or items through the use of situations is not, strictly speaking, a form of testing. The incident or situation item can be used to stimulate discussion and analysis. Therefore, the situation-type item can be one of the most valuable tools for measuring a trainee's ability to make application of things learned.

An example requiring a simple response. A claimant reports to the local office to refile a claim and states he has temporarily moved into the area served by the local office. What action should the receptionist take? The local office? The former area office?

An example requiring a detailed response. Jim Ellis, Production Manager, read a purchase request from the supervisor of inventory control, George Garrett. The request was for the purchase of new storage bins for the stockroom. Ellis called Garrett on the telephone, and after referring to the purchase request form said, "George, before I can consider your request, I need to know what the return on investment [ROI] is."

Garrett replied, "How can I calculate ROI on something like storage bins? If we were talking about a machine producing something, it would be possible. I just don't see how to evaluate an item of this type. We need more storage."

"Well, you better figure out a way," barked Ellis. "I'm not going to approve this until I can evaluate it. In fact, from now on, all requests for equipment will have to have a three-year ROI, or they will be turned down. I expect proof, not just claims." With that closing remark, Ellis hung up the telephone.

Questions:

1. What is your opinion of the Ellis approach?
2. Do you agree that a ROI calculation is impossible for storage bins? If not, how would you calculate ROI?

   Note: Rewrite these questions if you use this incident in group discussion.

A more complex example:

CHOOSING SIDES: A CASE OF AN AMBITIOUS MANAGER

Wait till you hear the news," Charlie told his wife when he came in from work Friday evening.

"What is it? Did they give you another raise in pay!"

"Isn't it enough that I'm the youngest plant manager the company has ever had? But you may not be too far off. It's not a raise, but listen to this. McBride, v.p. and controller; and Janssen, the engineering v.p.; and Brown, the assistant to the president, have invited me to go sailing with them on Saturday—tomorrow."

"Sailing?" she replied. "What do you know about sailing?"

"Nothing! But that's beside the point. Something tells me that I'd better develop an interest in sailing. All those guys have sailboats—big ones, I understand." Charlie paused, "Honey, what do you suppose it means? Why the sudden intense interest in me on their part?" Charlie really didn't expect an answer and continued. "Old Watkins had my job for twenty years, and as far as I can find out, nobody up top ever asked him out for so much as a drink. I've been plant manager nine months and look what happens!"

"Well, you'll know what it means tomorrow, won't you?" Doris said when Charlie finally paused.

*

Sailing was great. There was just enough wind. The weather was perfect. Everything went well. Charlie felt he had handled himself perfectly aboard, even if the chores had been rather simple. Charlie enjoyed the feeling that he fitted in easily with these men. He knew they liked him and that he had gained their respect.

A memorable day, Charlie told himself as they tied the boat to the slip. It was just beginning and it *would* be memorable.

The president's executive assistant poured a round of drinks. Looking straight at Charlie, he said, "The point is that by the time Burns realizes what harm Ellis is doing, there just isn't going to be anything left of this company." Brown pointed the drink at Charlie rather than hand it to him. "You, yourself, said that plant is in turmoil because of Ellis's new production methods."

"Well. . . ." Charlie was caught a little off guard. "You get that any time you introduce anything new. And we are in our peak season." Charlie began to feel he was making alibis if not defending his new boss outright.

Janssen leaned into the conversation, waving a finger. "That's precisely it! What kind of manufacturing executive comes in to a company from the outside, knowing nothing about the workers, nothing about the atmosphere of the place, and pushes through a raft of innovations just before we go into our heaviest production schedule?"

"There you are!" burst out McBride as he got up to freshen his drink. "Our competitive situation has been precarious for the past couple of years. It's nothing that won't change if we don't change. We've got a great line. No other manufacturer in our field can touch us. We can't risk production snafus."

Charlie was beginning to think that snafus were just what they were asking him to create. All three of these key executives seem to want one thing: Charlie's cooperation in helping to sabotage his new boss, Rodger Ellis.

Why? Charlie asked himself. He wasn't up to this kind of top management politics. But he knew that Burns, the firm's president, had acted for years as though Brown were his heir apparent. In the nine years since Charlie had joined the company, he'd picked up enough to realize that Brown, Janssen, and McBride ran things with no real interference from the other top executives.

Obviously, that had changed with Ellis coming aboard. Ellis was a hard-driving efficiency expert. Full of ideas that appealed to Charlie. Charlie felt that Ellis's ideas appealed to Burns. It was apparent that these three executives were extremely worried about Ellis's influence with the president. They were worried enough to reach down and ask Charlie to join them in a campaign to push Ellis out of the company.

Charlie's part in the scheme was to be extra zealous in carrying out Ellis's orders, enough so that morale would drop and some employees would begin to make mistakes. Nothing was to go out that didn't live up to the company's high standards, but there would be costly delays. As part of the plan, Charlie was to stop acting as a buffer. Ellis had a way of riling people. Without Charlie to calm the storms he would surely create, it wouldn't take much time for some of the employees to mutiny.

Charlie didn't like the scheme one bit. If he went along with it, Brown, McBride, and Janssen implied they would see to it that Charlie took over as manufacturing v.p. If he didn't go along with them, they need not hint what could happen. Charlie now knew too much.

"Of course, we don't expect an answer this minute," Brown said as they walked through the marina parking lot to their respective cars. "What say we all get together for lunch at the club next Wednesday?"

* * * *

Questions:

1. What's Charlie to do? Sabotage his boss or antagonize three of the most powerful company executives?

2. Are there other alternatives?
3. What advice would you give Charlie?

The situation test item method requires trainees to participate actively in application of selected principles and effectively stimulate conditions the trainees might encounter outside the classroom.

The situation test item method require trainees to participate actively in real or hypothetical problem situations and attempts to have trainees solve problems by applying sound principles developed through analytical thinking.

There are five steps in preparing a situation or case study.

1. Establish the specific objectives for the case study or situation.
2. List the desired learning outcomes.
3. Identify a problem or situation to be solved.
4. State the facts and conditions surrounding the problem (situation).
5. Prepare a clear statement of the problem (it may be done in story form).

The steps in conducting the case or situation methods are:

1. Prepare trainees for discussion and hand out the case.
2. Introduce the situation.
3. Establish roles, as required.
4. Motivate trainees to participate.
5. Review the facts and conditions.
6. Obtain group agreement on statement of the problem.
7. Supply additional facts and conditions, as required.
8. Start discussion on the case at hand.
9. Guide group discussion; keep it on the track.
10. Summarize, question, and guide until the desired lesson objectives are satisfied.
11. Summarize group recommendations and establish closure.

SUMMARY

Oral examinations can be used for teaching or review purposes, little or no grading weight should be given to the procedure. An oral question must be selected, worded, and used according to the purpose in asking. The following are excellent uses of oral questions to:

- Obtain trainee attention.
- Arouse interest.
- Open discussion.
- Provoke thinking.
- Accumulate data.
- Distribute discussion.

- Limit or end discussion.
- Elicit participation from the slower trainees.
- Arrive at conclusions.
- Develop a subject.
- Direct observation.
- Discover the trainees' weaknesses.
- Check understanding.
- Change discussion trends.
- Stimulate study.
- Review topics previously covered.
- Evaluate how well the group has grasped the new concepts, ideas, and facts.

When developing key oral questions, the instructor should consider the following:

1. Questions should challenge the trainee.
2. Account for individual differences.
3. Make the wording definite, clear, and concise.
4. Make each question center on only one idea.
5. Emphasize an understanding of relationships rather than memorization of facts.
6. Phrase the questions to indicate their purpose and the type of response desired (for example: list, classify, compare, criticize, define, explain, justify, summarize).

When a instructor uses the oral questioning technique, the following are a must:

1. Distribute questions fairly among the trainees.
2. Do not call on the trainees in a fixed order.
3. Allow time for answering.
4. Force each trainee to consider and evaluate every question and answer.
5. Hold repetition of a question to a minimum.
6. Commend good answers.
7. Use oral questions to keep trainees alert.
8. Do not permit group answers.

Good oral questions should:

- Be easily understood.
- Be composed of common words.
- Be thought provoking.
- Cover major points of the lesson.

There are some cautions when using the oral questioning technique. The instructor should avoid:

- Catch questions.
- Irrelevant questions.

- Leading questions.
- Pumping questions to get a response.

The steps in the oral questioning technique are:

1. Ask the question.
2. Pause to let all the trainees have time to think of an answer.
3. Call on the trainees by name.
4. Listen to a trainee's answer.
5. Repeat and emphasize the correct answer, as necessary.

There are several special advantages to the oral evaluation technique. Oral questioning permits the instructor to maintain a flexible procedure throughout the training program. Instructors may adapt the questions to fit individual backgrounds. New questions may be constructed on the spot, based upon the responses of the trainees; this flexibility is highly desirable in an active learning environment. Skillfull questioning may assist individuals to see implications in related situations not heretofore recognized. Generally speaking, less time is required to prepare questions to be used orally, although planning is a must.

> *Remember:* good oral questions don't just happen . . . they are planned.

Two-Option Alternate-Response Test Items

5

The most common form for alternate-response items is the statement to be judged true or false. True–false items are sentence-length statements to which the learner responds, indicating their truth or falsity. Plus–zero (+, 0) is a different form of the true–false question. Agree–disagree items ask the participants to indicate whether they agree or disagree with statements that cannot be considered either true or false with certainty. These items are used to measure attitudes.

The popularity of the two-option, alternate-response type of questions is due to the relative ease with which such items can be composed. In addition, true–false examinations can be administered rapidly and are easily scored.

These are several suggestions that should be heeded when devising two-option questions.

1. Limit each statement to a single idea. Do not use complex sentences, especially ones that might contain both true and false elements.

Poor:

T F   Before beginning the class, the instructor should make certain that all training aids are ready for use. There is no greater destroyer of class moral than an instructor who is fumbling with a chart not properly hung, struggling with equipment not ready for demonstration purposes, or discovering a film that is not properly set up in the classroom.

An *Improved* version will not be suggested since almost anything would be an improvement. The answer to the example is evident even to someone who knows nothing about instructor effectiveness. Therefore, such a test item measures nothing.

Poor:

T F   Theory X recognizes the interdependence of managers and employees, and Theory Y relies heavily on self-control and self-direction.

Improved:

T F   Theory X recognizes the interdependence of managers and employees.

T F   Theory Y relies heavily on self-control and self-direction.

> *Important:* Always review to eliminate long, complex, sentences.
> It is better to test for one single idea or fact.

Poor:

T F   Clean, white cotton gloves should always be worn when handling the adhesive or the cleaned surface or both. A fingerprint on a surface to be bonded can cause an area of low strength bonding; therefore, neither the bonding nor the faying surface nor the adhesive should be handled with the ungloved hand.

An uninformed individual as well as an informed adhesive-bonding trainee can give only one answer to such a lengthy, complex statement.

Improved:

T F   Clean, white cotton gloves must be worn while handling the adhesive during the bonding process.

T F   Since a fingerprint on a cleaned surface can cause an area of low strength bonding, the wearing of clean, white cotton gloves is a must.

> *Note:* Notice that the negative parts of the statement were omitted.

2. Avoid the use of specific determiners. Words such as "all," "never," "no," and "always" are more likely to be found in statements that are false than in true ones. Test-wise people soon realize this fact and make educated guesses that statements containing them are false without further thought about the item. By the same token, testees usually come to realize that cautiously worded statements employing such words as "frequently,"

"usually," "generally," and "most of the time" are likely to be true. Thus, it is better practice avoiding the use of specific determiners.

3. Make sure statements are unequivocally true or false. An ambiguous statement is more likely to be frustrating to the knowledgeable person than to the less knowledgeable person.

Poor:

T F   People see the attainment of their own needs linked with the goals of the company.

The well-informed individual would wonder how to mark such a statement. The statement is true from Theory Y manager's viewpoint. Yet if the manager is Theory X oriented, the statement is false. Statements must be composed in such a fashion so that someone knowledgeable in the subject matter can judge them to be unequivocally true or false.

Improved:

T F   When managers believe employees see the attainment of their own needs linked with the goals of the company, they are said to be managing with a Theory Y approach.

Poor:

T F   Over 223,000 new managers will be needed next year.

The reader may find it difficult to believe, but the author found the above true–false item in the Suggested Test Questions section of an instructor's manual for a management textbook. The question *does* fit the criterion that statements be unequivocally true or false. But could there be any other answer to this true–false item than *true*? It is best not to include this kind of statement as a test item.

4. When a controversial statement is used, the authority should be quoted. What is controversial to one person may not be to another. Sometimes an instructor may be too close to the subject to consider what is controversial.

Poor:

T F   A significant development in motivation was the distinction drawn between motivational and maintenance factors in the job situation.

It should be obvious to most management-development specialists that the above item is testing job motivation factors according to Frederick Herzberg. But a trainee could justify a false answer by stating that Abraham Maslow's hierarchy of needs had a profound influence on management thinking in job situation human relations years before Herzberg's theory appeared.

Improved:

T F According the Herzberg, the distinction between motivational and maintenance factors gives management a better chance of influencing employee motivation in a job situation.

T F Maslow believed that man is motivated to act by interrelated and interacting needs that are hierarchical in character.

Including the authority in the statement permits the individual taking the test to judge the correctness or incorrectness of the statement from their knowledge of an authority's stand.

5. Avoid the use of negative statements. More errors are made in response to negatively phrased items and more time is required to answer a negatively phrased item than for a positively phrased item. Some test takers may not notice the use of the negative, while others may become frustrated at having to deal with its semantic tangle. A negatively phrased item that may be false presents an ever greater difficulty for the trainee.

Poor:

T F Neither the bonding nor faying surfaces nor the adhesive should be handled with the ungloved hand.

Since the object of the item is to test the individual's knowledge of the adhesive bonding procedure rather than an understanding of semantics, couching the item in negative terms introduces a potential source of error.

Improved:

T F Clean, white cotton gloves must be worn when handling bonding and faying surfaces as well as the adhesive.

6. Try to use an approximately equal number of true and false statements. If trainees know that an instructor has included an approximately equal balance of true and false items, there ought to be less of a tendency for them to develop test-taking habits of marking either most items true or most items false. In addition, a pattern of answers should be avoided. Sometimes an alternate–response test includes a pattern, such as three true, one false, three true, one false. To avoid this, the instructor should consciously vary the proportion and arrangement of the items, check the arrangement by preparing an answer key, and rearranging items as required.

THE WEAKNESSES OF ALTERNATE-RESPONSE ITEMS

One weakness of an alternate–response item is the fact that it encourages the trainee to guess because they are poorly constructed. Many instructors select most items directly from text material as direct quotes, with the instructor failing to spend sufficient time on planning and refining. In addition, it is difficult to construct alternate-response items that are completely true or completely false. The alternate-response technique is not a testing method to be used with controversial subject matter.

THE ADVANTAGES OF ALTERNATE-RESPONSE ITEMS

Alternate-response test items can be a value measurement tool when they are carefully constructed. They are purely objective and lend themselves to easy and rapid scoring. They can be used to measure reasoning as well as memory. Since alternate-response tests can be taken rapidly, they allow extensive coverage of the subject matter to be evaluated.

SUMMARY

Here are some suggestions for construction of alternate-response items:

1. Use good grammar.
2. Avoid using trick or catch questions.
3. Prepare approximately the same number of true statements as false statements. Mix them thoroughly and do not set an answer pattern.
4. Make each item either all true or all false.
5. Do not make the true-statements consistently longer than the false ones.
6. Avoid negative statements.
7. Never use double negatives.
8. Use short, clear sentences.
9. Choose simple everyday words.
10. Do not use an item that suggests the answer to another item.

6 Multiple-Choice Test Items

The most popular type of objective test item is that in which the individual is required to choose one alternative response from a group of problems, questions or statements. This type of quiz is called a multiple-choice test. An example of a multiple-choice item is:

When rigging the aircraft canopy jettison system, you must first:

a. Raise the pilot seat leg braces.
b. Pull the external D-handle.
c. Pull the canopy T-handle.
d. Be sure initiators are safetied.
e. Remove the canopy jettison safety pin.

The multiple-choice item is considered the best type of objective testing method for measuring a variety of training objectives. Multiple-choice items either begin with an incomplete sentence, as in the example above, or are a question, such as: "What means should be taken to prevent repetition of costly mistakes?" Both of these are referred to as the problem or the premise.

The following are examples of two ways to write the same multiple-choice item:

1. *Statement to be completed.*
   The "exceptional release" on the DD Form 781–2 may be signed by the:
   a. crew chief.
   b. flight engineer.
   c. line chief.
   d. pilot.
2. *Question to be answered.*
   Who may sign the exceptional release on the DD Form 781–2?
   a. Crew chief.
   b. Flight engineer.
   c. Line chief.
   d. Pilot.

It does not matter whether the problem is stated in the form of an incomplete sentence or a question. Most test item writers prefer the incomplete sentence for two reasons.

1. It can save space both in the problem and listing the alternatives to be chosen.
2. If well constructed, it permits a smooth transition from reading the problem to seeking the correct alternative.

The potential disadvantage of the incomplete statement is that, if the instructor is not careful, some of the alternatives may be phrased so that they do not follow grammatically or make awkward sentences. The versatility of the multiple-choice item permits the testing of many principles of learning. To save space, only the correct response is given for each of the examples that follow.

1. *Definitions*
   A participle is the only verbal whose use is limited to:
   being a modifier.
2. *Skills*
   If the full-scale deflection of a 0–1 ma meter is to be increased to 0–2 ma, what is the value of the shunt resistor used? (Meter resistance = 50 ohms.)
   50 ohms.
3. *Facts*
   At sea level in an open container, the boiling point of water is:
   212° F.
4. *Reasoning*
   Ten bricks are placed on one end of a lever and two bricks on the

other end. To make the two bricks balance the ten bricks, the fulcrum must be:

between the center and the ten bricks.

5. *Purpose*

Which one of the following functions is usually performed by staff personnel?

inspection.

6. *Interpretation*

Soda pop fizzes because it contains:

carbon dioxide gas.

7. *Cause*

One of the causes of low strength bonding is:

touching the surface with an ungloved hand.

8. *Application of principle*

The law that states "for every action there is an equal and opposite reaction" explains why:

rocket motors can supply thrust above the atmosphere.

9. *Association*

Tornadoes and hurricanes most frequently occur when:

warm and cold air masses collide.

10. *Implication*

The switch in consumer spending from goods to services hinders:

the continued growth of industry.

11. *Troubleshooting analysis (used with electrical schematics or wiring diagrams)*

In the circuit diagram given, the resistance bridge is a Wheatstone type. Determine its internal DC resistance if the decade box is set on 300 ohms and the galvanometer reads zero.

Rx = 450 ohms.

12. *Research (used in handbooks or other reference materials)*

According to the *Supervisor's Accident Prevention Guide,* what three essential elements should you have to complete Form 33–19?

what happened, why it happened, and what corrective action is necessary.

These are only a few of the many kinds of learning principles that can be tested with multiple-choice items. Multiple-choice items are also relatively free of some of the ills that beset other types of objective test items. Unlike true–false items, multiple-choice items do not require one alternative to be *absolutely* correct. With multiple-choice items, the requirement is for *one of the alternatives to be markedly better than the others.* Multiple-choice items are relatively immune to test-taking habits. Because there usually are four or five alternatives to choose from on a multiple-choice item, they are not influenced by guessing to the same extent that true-false items are. On a true–

false item, the odds of obtaining the correct answer by chance alone are fifty-fifty. If there are five alternatives to a multiple-choice item, the odds are one in five of obtaining the correct answer by chance alone. These differences in probability make an important difference in the extent to which the two types of items are beset with measurement error.

Multiple-choice items are not subject to the same amount of ambiguity as fill-in items. Also, because multiple-choice items rest on the principle of selecting the best alternative rather than supplying one which is absolutely correct, the problem premise need not be specified as elaborately as is required with fill-ins. It is usually easier to test more complex aspects of learning with multiple-choice items.

The multiple-choice technique is a versatile testing method that requires discriminatory thinking on the part of the test taker. Multiple-choice items are sometimes varied by making all of the choices correct and requiring the test taker to select the best choice.

Unless instructors feel much more comfortable with other types of objective items or they feel that the subject matter requires other types of objective items, it is strongly recommended that multiple-choice techniques be employed for most objectives tests.

ANATOMY OF MULTIPLE-CHOICE ITEMS

The parts that go together to make a multiple-choice item are:

Stem + Alternatives = Item

For example:

Stem ⟶ The instrument used to read resistance in an electrical circuit is:

Alternatives
    a. an ohmmeter. ⟵ *Desired Answer*
    b. a pitometer.
    c. a potentiometer.   *Distractors*
    d. a voltmeter.

Each multiple-choice item should be:

1. an important aspect of the instructional activity and/or the trainee's job.
2. specific, clear, and as brief as possible.
3. realistic and practical.
4. constructed to stress ability to reason rather than mere memory of facts.
5. a complete grammatical unit.

The *stem* should pose a problem. As stated earlier, the stem can be in the form of a direct question or an incomplete statement.

The *Alternatives* should be:

1. related to each other.
2. in ascending or descending order if a numerical response is asked for. The alternatives may be in any form that will fulfill the logical requirements of the stem. For example, the alternatives may be:

   - sentences
   - phrases
   - clauses
   - single words
   - letters
   - numbers
   - formulas
   - diagrams
   - schematics
   - pictures

The *desired answer* to a multiple-choice item should be:

1. the best possible answer.
2. independent of information given in other items on the test.

The *distracters* should be important, plausible choices rather than obviously wrong.

HINTS FOR WRITING MULTIPLE-CHOICE TEST ITEMS

This list of hints has been formulated for the construction of multiple-choice items. Only the most important ideas will be discussed. Most of the items illustrating the hints are concerned with the knowledge of content rather than levels of mental functioning in various subject areas.

1. The problem should clearly point to the theme of the correct alternative answer. A multiple-choice item should not merely present a collection of unrelated facts or ideas, one of which is true and the others false. Instead, a clear question should be posed by the problem or premise that can be reasonably answered by one, and only one, of the alternative choices listed.

Poor:

Good management practices consider:

a. due consideration of the number of people in the organization.
b. delegation of responsibility with the necessary authority.
c. that enough variety of work is provided to prevent boredom.
d. that the organizational chart is displayed prominently and that the chart is explained to all concerned.

When the statement of the problem begins with such a vague premise as good management practices, many different alternative responses could follow. Many times instructors state a similar problem as:

Which one of the following things is true of good management practices:

Unless the one *true* response and the remaining *false* alternatives are stated very precisely, the intended correct response does not follow logically from the premise. When the problem does not clearly point to the theme, the instructor is often required to write alternatives that are very long in order to make them precisely true or false.

Improved:

In order to assure effective operation of the organizational principle Unity of Command, the best step to be taken is to:

a. give due consideration to the number of subordinates reporting to a superior.
b. delegate authority with the necessary responsibility.
c. display an organization chart and explain it to all people concerned.
d. provide enough variety in assigned work to prevent boredom.

Now the problem premise clearly focuses on the Unity of Command. The qualification the best step to be taken further specifies the correct alternative sought by the test item.

2. Incorrect alternatives should be plausibly related to the problem. On some items, the incorrect alternatives are so completely unrelated to the problem that, even if the trainees know very little about the problem, they can rule out all but the correct alternative.

Poor:

The vessel that carries oxygenated blood from the heart to the body is called the:

a. trapezius muscle.
b. forebrain.
c. patella tendon.
d. ascending aorta.

Even if the trainees know little about the circulatory system, they probably know that muscles, tendons, and parts of the brain are not blood vessels. Consequently, they would rule out all but alternative "d."

Improved:

The vessel that carries oxygenated blood from the heart to the body is called the:

a. vena cava.
b. pulmonary artery.
c. femoral artery.
d. ascending aorta.

Now the item is somewhat more difficult. Increasing the homogeneity of the choices can also make a multiple-choice item more difficult.

Poor:

What does consistent mean?

a. Steady.
b. Unsteady.
c. Compatible.
d. Fluid.
e. Changeable.

Improved:

What does consistent mean?

a. Compatible.
b. Predictable.
c. Repetitious.
d. Revolving.
e. Steady.

Just by changing the choices, the above item becomes considerably more difficult. In addition, notice that the choices are listed alphabetically which also increases difficulty.

When constructing multiple-choice items involving arithmetic operations, it is particularly important that the incorrect alternatives be plausibly related to the problem. Typically, the distractors are solutions that would be obtained by following an erroneous procedure, e.g., subtracting instead of adding or forgetting to invert and then multiply.

The rule of thumb in composing alternative answers is that, to the individual who knows the answer, only one alternative is plausible; to the person who does not know the answer, all the alternatives look equally plausible.

3. Correct alternatives should not be consistently different in appearance

from incorrect alternatives. Only the knowledge of subject matter should provide clues about the correct alternative.

Poor:

a. 424° F.
b. 282° F.
c. 212° F at sea level, in an open container.
d. 98° F.

It was not necessary to include the premise in order to point the reader to the correct answer. Alternative "c" is so much longer and more detailed than the others that it is a dead give-away.

Improved:

The boiling point of water at sea level, in an open container, is:

a. 424° F.
b. 282° F.
c. 212° F.
d. 98° F.

The violation above was a rather obvious example of making the correct alternative look different from the others. In some test items, it is difficult to prevent the correct alternative from being longer and more highly specified than the incorrect alternatives. This does not necessarily provide unwanted clues if the correct alternative is not consistently different in appearance. To balance out such clues, some of the incorrect alternatives should be longer and more highly specified.

> *Important:* If the answer is a number, use all numbers. Rank the numbers in decreasing or increasing order. The boiling-point question above is a prime example.

Another example:

If a man earns $1,278.00 in 90 working days, in 75 working days he earns (assume no overtime or other premium pay):

a. $1,056.00
b. $1,056.20
c. $1,065.00
d. $1,103.00

4. All alternatives in the item must be grammatically consistent. Each alternative must be grammatically correct as the ending for the question or

premise stated. In addition, as many as possible of the words of the item should be included in the premise to avoid repetition in each alternative.

Poor:

Why do living organisms need oxygen?

a. To purify the blood.
b. To oxidize waste.
c. To release energy.
d. To assimilate food.
e. To fight infection.

Improved:

Living organisms need oxygen to:

a. purify blood.
b. oxidize waste.
c. release energy.
d. assimilate food.
e. fight infection.

5. Avoid grammatical cues and sentence structures that give away the correct alternative.

Poor:

A steel ball and a ball of cotton would fall at the same speed in a:

a. atmosphere.
b. vacuum.
c. any fluid.
d. gases.

To get the correct answer, trainees need know nothing about physics. The correct response cannot be atmosphere or any fluid because the premise ends in *a.* Since the sentence cannot grammatically end in *gases,* alternative "d" is also ruled out.

Poor:

The ground-control approach system is designed for directing aircraft in:

a. landing approaches.
b. climbing to different altitudes.
c. taking off from busy airstrips.
d. formation flying.

Improved:

The ground-control approach system is designed for directing aircraft in:

a. attacking.
b. bombing.
c. intercepting.
d. landing.

In the poor version, the word "approaches" in the choice of alternatives identifies it as the correct answer. In the improved version, all four operations are approaches, yet the word itself does not appear in the alternatives.

6. Avoid employing alternatives that say things like "none of the above," "both a and b above," "all of the above."

Poor:

Before using a stop countersink tool, the aircraft structures mechanic should:

a. Ask the tool crib attendant to set it properly.
b. Check the torque print on the depth setting.
c. Check the depth setting with scrap material.
d. None of the above.

If "none of the above" were not included as an alternative, alternative "c" would be the best choice. With "none of the above" included as an alternative, aircraft structures trainees are placed in a dilemma. They must decide what is absolutely correct. Consequently, the knowledgeable trainee asks, "What does the instructor want?"

Improved:

a. ask the tool crib attendant to set it properly.
b. check the torque point on the depth setting.
c. check the depth with scrap material.
d. Remove the countersink cage.

The use of "none of the above" and other such alternatives changes the basis for answering from one of seeking the most correct alternative to seeking one or more absolutely correct alternatives. This introduces all the difficulties found in true–false items. The use of "none of the above" and other such alternatives is definitely not recommended.

7. All choices should be plausible. If several of the choices are not plausible, the trainee's chances of guessing the correct response are increased.

Poor:

The end punctuation for an interrogative sentence is:

a. A colon.
b. A semicolon.
c. A comma.
d. A question mark.
e. An exclamation point.

Improved:

The end punctuation for an interrogative sentence is:

a. A period.
b. An exclamation point.
c. A question mark.
d. The ampersand.

8. Avoid including material in the problem that is unrelated to the theme of the intended response. The problem should be stated in sufficient detail to orient trainees to the desired response. However, if superfluous details are inserted in the problem, they can confuse trainees.

9. Use negatives sparingly in the premise statements. The negative multiple-choice item, just as the negative alternate-response item, tends to measure the trainees' reading ability. In some items, the only sensible course is to have trainees look for an alternative that does not apply or does not follow a specific form of a principle. If done sparingly, some use of the negative is permissible. The difficulty in using negatives is that they are somewhat confusing to test takers, who are more used to seeking correct answers than incorrect ones.

Poor:

Which one of the following does *not* normally appear in a small-group discussion outline?

a. The discussion's purpose.
b. Background information.
c. Drill-type questions.
d. Concluding remarks.

When you arrange the physical facilities for your small-group discussion, you, the leader, should *avoid* which of the following?

a. Furnishing ash trays for the participants.
b. Arranging seating so that all the participants can see each other.

c. Planning to sit apart from the group.

d. Arranging visual aids for easy viewing.

When possible, it is better to give positive rather than negative expressions of problems. When negatives must be used, make sure the negative word or phrase is underlined or in some way made clearly evident to the test taker.

> *Important:* By all means avoid the use of double negatives— negatives in both the problem and in some of the alternatives.

10. Avoid irrelevant sources of difficulty in the statement of the problem or in the alternatives. Items are supposed to be made difficult because of the subject matter being tested and not by irrelevant sources. This suggestion is the corollary of hints to 4 through 9 above.

Poor:

Vernier engines are designed according to missile design specifications. Subsequently, research and development test firings substantiate the design criteria for operating off the engine tank system so that:

a. the rated thrust of each engine is one thousand pounds, provided they are operating at maximum efficiency.

b. should malfunctions fail to appear, the combined thrust of both vernier engines should approximate close to six hundred and ninety pounds of pressure against the surrounding air.

c. seven hundred and fifty pounds of pressure are most likely to be the value of thrust felt from each engine.

d. should there be no malfunctions present, and providing all operating conditions are met, the poundage thrust must have a rating of approximately eight hundred and thirty per engine.

Improved:

When operating off the main engine tank system, each vernier engine should have a thrust rating of:

a. 690 lb.

b. 750 lb.

c. 830 lb.

d. 1000 lb.

> *Important:* Test items must be clearly stated and contain only the necessary information.

11. Each item should be independent of every other item. There are two

aspects of writing test items to which this suggestion relates. On the one hand, there is the rather obvious point that a problem as stated in one multiple-choice item should never give away the answer to another item. The converse of the problem of giving away the answer to an item is having the correct answer to one item depend upon responding correctly to a previous item. The author has known instructors who delighted in the fact that if trainees could not correctly solve the first problem, they were doomed to choose incorrect responses throughout the remainder of the test. Such instructors misunderstand the objective and purpose behind the evaluation of trainees.

Poor:

A manager followed this procedure in monitoring instruction: Step 1. Observe the class activities (return to office). Step 2. Review lesson plan and references on subject. Step 3. Write a report. Step 4. Critique the instructor. A correct sequence is:

a. as state above.
b. steps 1, 2, 4, 3.
c. steps 2, 1, 4, 3.
d. steps 2, 1, 3, 4.

The above question omits one important step in the best monitoring procedure. What is that step?

a. Evaluate the instruction.
b. Schedule follow-up action.
c. Inform the instructor in advance of the visit.
d. Discuss evaluation with the instructor's supervisor.

The main disadvantage to this technique is that it forces the reader to refer back to the previous question and alternatives within the item, which is time-consuming. As the string of interdependent questions grows longer, the technique becomes an extremely poor method of testing.

> *Important:* After a test has been constructed, it is a good idea to read it over very carefully to be sure that the principle of independence of items has not been inadvertently violated.

12. Alternatives within an item should not overlap or be synonymous with one another; they should be different but related to the premise. Overlapping or synonymous choices cause unnecessary confusion. An effort should also be made not to repeat the same or similar alternatives too often within a test. If a certain word or phrase reappears frequently, the test-wise trainee

soon comes to realize it probably is not the correct answer most of the time it appears.

13. Alternatives should be randomly ordered for each item. Test designers often unwittingly place the correct alternative more frequently in the middle of the list than in either the first or last positions. The best method of ordering alternatives is to do it randomly. After all the items have been constructed, go back and randomly distribute the correct choices so that each position is used approximately the same number of times. Many books on statistics contain tables of random numbers that can be used to order the alternatives randomly for each item.

14. Avoid confusing the multiple-choice testing style with other testing techniques. Many instructors create multiple-choice items to measure the objectives and trainee grasp of the subject matter. One of the popular test items constructions is to use the multiple-choice item as a true–false item.

Poor:

Which one of the following statements about the use of a supervisory checklist is false? It:

a. eliminates the need for an oral critique when a copy is sent to the instructor.
b. helps standardize supervisors' evaluations of instruction.
c. ensures that all major aspects of a rehearsal or class are observed.
d. tends to reduce nit-picking.

> *Important:* Add variety to the testing program. Use the information in this book to construct a variety of different styles of test items measuring the same subject matter and objectives.

15. Ensure that item content relates to important aspects of the subject matter. The final and most significant suggestion is to ensure that something worthwhile is being measured. No matter how faithfully instructors apply the other suggestions of item construction contained in this section, if their items are concerned only with trivial facts, nothing can be done to save the test.

> *Remember:* Tests must measure the objectives of the training. Always check for job relatedness!

SUMMARY

The advantages of multiple-choice test items can be summarized as follows. They:

- Are purely objective.
- Reduce guessing.
- Can be designed to test a variety of learning principles.
- Tend to be more reliable.

The disadvantages are that they:

- Tend to develop items that measure facts alone.
- Make it difficult to construct enough plausible alternatives.
- Consume a lot of space.

Here are some construction suggestions to keep in mind when constructing multiple-choice test items.

1. Four alternatives are recommended; five are considered maximum; use of less than three makes a true–false item.
2. Design alternatives so that most of them are plausible.
3. Avoid:
   a. Wording that serves as clues.
   b. Changes in parts of speech.
   c. Mixing singular and plurals.
   d. The use of "none of the above" or "all of the above."
4. Vary the position of the correct response to avoid creating a pattern of correct answers.
5. Make the alternatives as nearly equal in length as possible; be consistent; if the answer is a number, use all numbers.

7 Matching Test Items

Matching exercises are not widely used. Matching items are most useful for measuring selection or recognition. In a matching exercise, the learner is presented with two lists, of such things as symbols, pictures, names, words, facts, phrases, numbers, and principles. In a sense, matching is a series of interrelated multiple-choice items. It is the pairing of a term on one side with the term or terms on the other. In its simplest form, matching requires a series of multiple-option decisions by the learner. Here is a simple example of a matching exercise.

____ Theory X and Theory Y	a. Argyris
____ Management by objectives	b. Blake and Mouton
____ Maintenance and motivational	c. Herzberg
factors	d. Lippitt
____ Organization renewal	e. McGregor
____ Hierarchy of needs	f. Maslow
	g. Odiorne

Matching questions may be constructed by writing several statements in simple sentence form. For example:

1. The bucksaw is used to cut logs.
2. The coping saw is used to make curved cuts.
3. The hacksaw is used to cut metal.
4. The handsaw is used for ripping and cross cutting.
5. The keyhole saw is used to cut small holes in wood.
6. The miter saw is used to make angular cuts.
7. The pruning saw is used to cut branches.

After dividing the sentences into subject phrases and predicate phrases mixing the arrangement of each.

Poor:

1. The bucksaw is used   ( ) to cut branches
2. The coping saw is used   ( ) to make angular cuts
3. The hacksaw is used   ( ) to cut keys
4. The handsaw is used   ( ) to cut metal
5. The keyhole saw is used   ( ) to make curved cuts
6. The miter saw is used   ( ) to cut small holes in wood
7. The pruning saw is used   ( ) to cut logs

Improved:

Saws	Uses
____ buck	1. angular cuts
____ coping	2. cut keys
____ hack	3. cross cutting
____ hand	4. curved cuts
____ keyhole	5. cutting metal
____ miter	6. ripping
____ pruning	7. small holes in wood
	8. cutting logs
	9. cutting branches
	10. trimming shrubs

Matching sets are used well for the measurement of specific basic facts or knowledge. Matching items can be constructed so that the trainee has virtually no chance of guessing the correct responses.

The following are suggestions to assist the test designer in the construction of matching test items.

1. The list of options should be at least fifty percent longer than the list of items. If the two lists are of the same length, guessing plays too prominent a part in matching the items. If, in the example above, there were only five names on the right and trainees knew four correct matches, testees would get the fifth one free. If there were only six names on the right, they would have

a fifty-fifty chance of correctly matching the fifth item, even if they flipped a coin. Consequently, the list of options should be considerably longer to lessen the influence of guessing.

Poor:

Directions: Match each contribution to its initiator.

____ Company's and employee's goals integration	a. Fayol, Henri
____ 14 management principles	b. Follett, Mary
____ first to use interchangeable parts and	c. Gantt, Henry
assembly-line	d. Taylor, Frederick
____ scientific management	e. Whitney, Eli
____ visual planning techniques	

When the two columns are evenly matched, guessing plays a prominent part in the matching of the items.

Improved:
- a. Babbage, Charles
- b. Fayol, Henri
- c. Follett, Mary
- d. Ford, Henry
- e. Gantt, Henry
- f. Gilbreth, Frank and Lillian
- g. Taylor, Frederick
- h. Whitney, Eli

Increase this list of names on the right to eight plausible choices.

Note: The sets are listed alphabetically. See hint number 5.

2. The list of premise items should be relatively short. The premise list should not be less than five or more than ten. When lists are longer than this, learners get lost in scanning the two lists; they may make incorrect matchings purely because of clerical errors. As the length of the list increases beyond the maximum recommended, the time required to complete the matching goes up markedly. It is best to break up long lists into several shorter sets.

3. When a matching item consists of a word or phrase having many associations to be paired with a more specific word or phrase, the more specific term should be placed in the stem column. In effect, the stem column (left) asks a question, and the option column (right) provides the answer.

Premises should be in the left-hand column and responses in the right-hand column. For ease in scoring, the blank space for answering should precede the premise.

A good example

Column I	Column II
____ Benefit operations and data processing	a. Administrative compliance
	b. Benefit payment controls
____ Claims operations	c. Budget-cost studies
____ Determinations and hearings	d. Disqualifications determinations
____ Tax and accounting operations	e. Equipment application
	f. Financial controls
	g. Interstate benefits
	h. Principles of interpretation

4. All the entries in each list should relate to the same central theme. In the example illustrated in 1 above, it would have been poor practice to put Benjamin Franklin in the list of names because he clearly belongs to a different era and relates to different events. The instructor should avoid making a matching exercise a potpourri of dissimilar topics. Each exercise should have a central theme. It is important that homogeneous premises and homogeneous responses be grouped in each matching set.

5. Premises and response sets should be arranged alphabetically, chronologically, or numerically. All tests should be constructed for the convenience of the test takers. Matching items are no exception. When responses are arranged as recommended, the trainee who knows the answers can locate them with ease without frequent reading of the entire list.

Poor:

Directions: Match the location of regional offices.

Office	Location
____ Region IX	a. Chicago
____ Region IV	b. Boston
____ Region II	c. Chambersburg
____ Region I	d. Kansas City
____ Region III	e. Atlanta
____ Region VI	f. Dallas
	g. Cleveland
	h. New York
	i. Denver

Improved:

Regional Office	Location
____ I	a. Atlanta
____ II	b. Boston
____ III	c. Chambersburg
____ IV	d. Chicago
____ V	e. Cleveland
____ VI	f. Dallas
	g. Denver
	h. Kansas City
	i. New York

6. All items of the matching set must be included on the same page. A trainee may become confused if part of the matching set appears on another page, because reading is complicated by such an arrangement.

7. Test instructions should clearly state how the matching is to be performed. Learners should be told whether they are to locate something an individual did, facts that relate to principles, definitions of terms, or whatever else is at issue. In particular, learners should be told whether more than one match is to be made for each entry or whether an entry on one list can be matched with more than one entry in the other list. Generally, it is better to avoid both of these practices and to require that only one match be made for each entry. The following directions are for the example in 3 above.

Directions: In the two columns below are listed organizational units and some of the functions for which they are responsible. The task is to classify the items in column I under the items in column II. More than one item in column I matches the items in column II.

Matching sets can be of the identification-type test item to measure trainee ability to recall and give the proper names to such things as symbols, pictures, specific parts, mechanical units, electronic units, and tools.

Directions: A few of the commonest forms of sawteeth are shown in column B. Match their numbers with the names of the sawteeth in column A. Some names may have more than one number.

A	B
____ Tenon	
____ Mill	
____ Ripsaw	
____ Lance	
____ American	
____ Champion	
____ Fleam	
____ Groving	
____ Diamond	
____ Lightning	

Customarily, the matching item is used when there are many simple facts, dates, names, and definitions to be remembered. However, the matching item can test more complex mental processes, as well.

EXAMPLES:

Abstract Reasoning.

The four "problem figures" in each row make a series. Find which one of the "answer figures" would be the next, or the fifth one in the series.

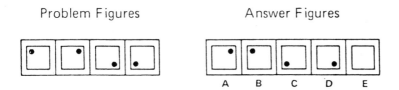

Problem Figures   Answer Figures

A   B   C   D   E

Mechanical Reasoning.

Which man has the heavier load?

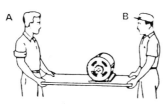

Space Relations.

Which one of the following figures could be made by folding the given pattern? The pattern always shows the outside of the figure.

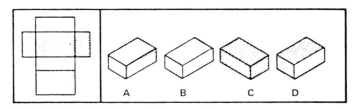

SUMMARY

The advantages of matching test items are that they are:

- Purely objective.

- Easy to construct.
- Easily and rapidly scored.
- Reliable and discriminating.
- Measure factual knowledge and judgment.
- Measure a trainee's ability to recognize relationships and make associations.

Their disadvantages are that:

- Many areas of subject matter cannot be tested with this method.
- They provide a poor measure of interpretation and understanding.
- Items can be answered by the process of elimination if too few pairs are used.
- They are likely to contain irrelevant clues to correct responses.

Here are suggestions for construction of matching test items.

1. The premise list should not be less than five or more than ten items long; if fewer than five are used, guessing results; if more than ten are used; the question becomes too time-consuming.
2. Include at least three more items in the answer column than in the question column.
3. Place the column containing the longer phrases or clauses on the right side of the page.
4. Do not include obviously out-of-place words in the answer column.
5. Avoid clues that mix the use of singular and plural words in opposite columns.
6. List nothing in either column that is not relevant to the subject.
7. State in the directions the area of instructions to which the items listed apply.

8 Completion or Fill-in Items

Alternate-response, true–false, multiple-choice, and matching test questions are selection or recognition types. In answering these exam forms, learners are reacting to information or misinformation put before them rather than depending on their memory for the responses given. In responding to completion or fill-in questions, learners must recall, compute or otherwise create the answers. In the most popular completion type of question, the learner extends or adds to the test by writing words, phrases, numbers, or symbols in the spaces provided.

One might say that the fill-in item is actually a very short essay item; rather than choosing from among given alternatives, the trainee must supply the correct answer. The fill-in item is most useful when the knowledge of many simple facts is to be be tested. For example:

1. *Incomplete sentence*
   The assignment of personnel in a suitable manner for accomplishing the objective of a plan is the _____ function of management.
2. *Definition*
   Define the Law of Unity of Command.

   _____

   _____

3. *Question*
   What is the chemical notation for liquid bleach?

   _____

4. *Recall*
   The four principles of organization are:
   1. _____
   2. _____
   3. _____
   4. _____

5. *Skill*

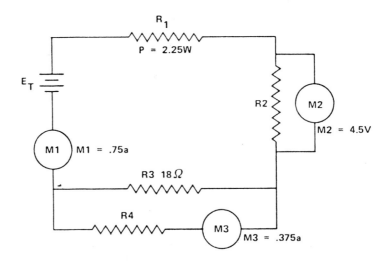

Give the value for each item on the above schematic.

E_T	_____	E_{R1}	_____
I_T	_____	I_{R1}	_____
R_T	_____	R_1	_____
P_T	_____	P_{R1}	_____
E_{R2}	_____	E_{R3}	_____
I_{R2}	_____	I_{R3}	_____
R_2	_____	R_3	_____
P_{R2}	_____	P_{R3}	_____

Show all calculations on the back of this page.

LISTING OR ENUMERATION ITEMS

The listing or enumeration test item requires trainees to supply a list of terms, rules, or factors. Trainees should not be required to list items in a particular order or sequence, unless there is only one sequence. The listing test item measures the degree of recall of very specific points of information.

Example: List six characteristics of a good test.

1. _____   4. _____
2. _____   5. _____
3. _____   6. _____

The listing-type item tends to be somewhat subjective and can place too much emphasis on memorizing facts. But this type of item reduces guessing and allows for some freedom of expression.

Hints for construction of listing or enumeration test items:

1. Design each item to call for specific facts.
2. Make sure the items to be listed involve only a few words.
3. Restrict the question so that no more than six to eight items are required to be listed.
4. Do not use this method if the trainee can choose from a large variety of possible responses.

COMPLETION ITEMS

Completion test items require the learner to recall and supply definite and exact information. A completion item consists of incomplete statements in which one or more keywords have been omitted. The words, when placed in the appropriate blanks, make the statement complete and meaningful. Completion questions and short-answer quizzes have a wide range of application in measuring recall, provided the test items are carefully constructed. Listed below are some important hints to be followed in constructing these type of test items.

1. Only significant words should be omitted, otherwise the item will not contribute to the measurement of specific training objectives.

Example: The law of inertia states that a body at rest tends to remain at rest and a body in motion tends to remain in motion.

In almost every training program involving rockets or jet engines, Newton's laws of motion are discussed and tested. In the above example, leaving out the word "inertia" would test recognition of the law. Leaving out the two "at rest" phrases or the two "in motion" phrases would test rote memory. Leaving out the words "law" or "body" would be of little significant value to the measurement of the lesson's objectives.

2. As a rule, use only one or two blank spaces. When more than two blanks are used, as described in the item above, ambiguity is likely to be a

problem. An item calling for more than three blanks may, of course, be used legitimately if it is constructed with caution.

Example: The three elements which are essential for combustion are _____ , _____ , and _____ .

> *Note:* The reason why multiple blanks are legitimate in this case is because there are three elements that must be present in order to have combustion.

3. Make sure only one term will sensibly complete the statement or answer the question.

Poor:

The liquid oxygen rapid transfer valve is located _____ .

In addition to the intended answer, an equally reasonable fill-in would be "outside," "with difficulty," and "by the lowest ranking member of the maintenance team."

Another example of a fill-in item in which numerous responses would be correct is:

Oxygen is essential for _____ .

Equally good responses would be "combustion," "life on earth," "submarine crews," or "the PLSS Apollo backpack."

The two examples above are rather obvious instances in which the intended response is ambiguous. Instructors often subtly mislead learners in regard to which answer should be inserted. At fault usually is the fact that instructors fail to add sufficient details to pinpoint the correct answer. After the test is administered the instructors often learn from the trainee responses that more than one answer can probably be inserted. This is how instructors gradually learn how to write less ambiguous fill-in items.

If too many clues are given in the item, most trainees will answer correctly, but the item will be too easy to provide a valid measurement. If too few clues are given, a great variety of answers can be given because of the failure to understand what response was desired. Again, valid measurement is limited.

4. When omitting words to make incomplete statements, leave enough clues so that the individuals who know the correct response can write it in the space provided.

Poor:

The proper organization will provide _____ _____ _____ _____ correct _____ _____ _____ ; and _____ _____ for every person in the group.

It is very doubtful that individuals knowing correct response can fill in the above blanks. This example illustrates another trap these instructors fall into who believe that, by breaking the line, the testee will be clued as to the number of words in the correct response. If anything breaking up the blanks tends to confuse rather than facilitate answering.

The following is an example of omission of a different type. Notice that there are enough clues so that the knowledgeable trainee can fill in the missing circuit.

Directions: On this sheet complete the missing coupling networks within the dashed lines. No connections except those indicated are to extend through the dashed lines.

COUPLING NETWORK

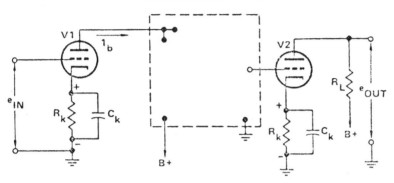

L-C-R COUPLED AMPLIFIER USING TRIODES

5. Place the blank space near the end of the sentence to make the task easier and to avoid the trainees having to work backward for the answer.

Poor:

In the internal combustion engine, the _____ converts the straight-line motion of the pistons into the circular motion of the drive shaft.

Improved:

In the internal combustion engine, the straight-line motion of the pistons is converted into the circular motion of the drive shaft by the _____ .

Not only does placing the blank at the end of the statement aid the trainee, it can also simplify the scoring procedure for the instructor.

Poor:

a. _____ is used to prevent oxidation during welding.
b. _____ is the number of cubic inches in a U.S. gallon.
c. The _____ primary function is to prevent shavings from sticking in the throat of the plane.
d. The _____ wrench is used to measure the amount of twisting force being applied to a nut.

Improved:

a. To prevent oxidation during welding, _____ is used.
b. The number of cubic inches in a U.S. gallon is _____ .
c. To prevent shavings from sticking in the throat of the plane is the primary function of the _____ .
d. The wrench used to measure the amount of twisting force being applied to a nut is called a _____ .

6. Avoid repeating textbook phrasing word for word. It places too much reliance by the learner on rote memorization.

Poor:

According to the text, there are _____ direct relationships and _____ direct and cross relationships in an organization composed of one supervisor and six subordinates.

7. Avoid grammatical clues to the correct answer.

The end punctuation for an interrogative sentence is an _____ mark.

Improved:

The end punctuation for an interrogative sentence is a(n) _____ .

8. Use completion-type item only when appropriate. Do not use completion items when another method of testing would be better.

Poor:

Management should ____, ____, ____, ____, and ____ while the worker carries out the remainder of the work.

The instructor is testing for the following topics covered in management training:

topic	*answer desired above*
planning	(plan)
organizing	(organize)
directing	(direct)
controlling	(control)
motivating	(motivate)

There are a variety of test items that would measure the trainee's understanding of the five managerial functions better than a mere listing of the functions.

Poor:

a. The (Clayton) Act legalized strikes and pickets.
b. The (Wagner) Act gave unions the right to bargain.

c. The (Landrum-Griffin) Act regulated union elections.

d. The (Taft-Hartley) Act gave the right to opt for an open shop or a union shop.

f. The (Sherman) Act held that unions were conspiracies in restraint of trade.

Improved:

Since the above example is more of a matching exercise than anything else, why not test the above with a match set of items?

Important features	Laws
____ ruled unions are conspiracies	a. Clayton Act
____ legalized strikes and pickets	b. Landrum-Griffin Act
____ gave unions to right to bargain	c. Norris-LaGuardia Act
____ regulated union elections	d. Sherman Act
____ gave the right to an open vs. a union shop	e. Smith-Hughes Act
	f. Taft-Hartley Act
	g. Wagner Act

Important: Relying solely on completion items makes it difficult to measure higher levels of understanding.

Completion items can be used in paragraph form to test continuous thought within a specific subject matter area. Completion items can also be used to guide trainees through reference materials, manuals, tables, policies, procedures, and specifications. In this way, completion items become a teaching tool.

EXAMPLE: Assumes the trainee has a copy of the specification manual.

Directions: The following are incomplete statements. Complete each by writing the correct word, phrases, or numbers in the blanks provided. The information is based on material contained in Process Specification 14240. Use the process specifications as needed.

1. A minimum period of _____ hours should elapse between removal of adhesive from _____ degree storage.

2. Refrigerators used for adhesive primers must operate at _____ degrees or lower.

3. The uncured graphite/epoxy prepreg material shall be limited to _____ cumulative hours at a temperature up to _____ °F.

4. Apply primer to titanium parts with a _____ and allow a dry film thickness of _____ to _____ for BR 400 and/or a thickness of _____ to _____ for BR 127.

5. The three alternatives for a clean surface for curing fixtures are _____, _____, or _____.

6. While handling adhesives and cleaned detail parts, it is mandatory to wear a clean _____ .

7. Metal dams shall be coated with _____ .

8. The cured ply thickness of MMS-549 type I is _____, for MMS-548 it is _____, and for MMS-546 it is _____ .

9. The minimum number of thermocouples per part is/are _____ .

10. During heatup, the autoclave free air temperature should not exceed _____ .

11. During initial heatup, raise part temperature to _____ 10°F in _____ minutes.

12. Pressure during initial heatup should be held at _____ PSIG.

SUMMARY

The advantages in using completion or fill-in items are that they are:

- Effective in measuring recall.
- Relatively easy to prepare.
- Sample a wide range of subject matter.
- Discriminate effectively.
- Short *natural* form of question.
- Free from guessing, if constructed properly.

Their disadvantages are that:

- They are hard to construct by purely objective criteria.
- They tend to measure verbal ability and the memorizing of facts rather than application.
- Completion items are somewhat unrealistic.
- Relying solely on fill-in items makes it difficult to measure higher levels of understanding.
- It is extremely difficult to construct items that call for only one correct response.
- Continued use encourages trainees to spend time memorizing trivial details rather than seeking more important understanding.
- There is a tendency for instructors to leave too many blanks.
- They usually have to be scored by the instructor who taught the subject matter.

Here are some suggestions for construction of fill-in or completion test items.

1. Do not copy statements directly from the text studied by the trainees.
2. Write out a number of important factual statements based on the objectives of the instruction.

3. Do not start a question or statement with a blank.
4. Omit only key or critical words.
5. Never omit verbs.
6. Avoid leaving a large number of blanks. Omit no more than three words in a sentence. A short statement with only one word omitted is preferable.
7. Make all blanks the same length regardless of the length of the omitted words to avoid giving clues.
8. Make each blank call for a single idea.
9. Place the blanks near the end of the sentence.
10. Make the statement complete enough to eliminate doubt as to its meaning.

9 Performance Testing

The objective of virtually all employee development activities is to train the employee to do something new. The instructor in business and industry training must also show as well as tell. Since the prime purpose of training is to create in employees the ability to put knowledge into practice on the job, the degree of skill acquired needs to be measured. Acquired skill can be assessed rather accurately with performance tests. In addition, performance testing is the natural end-item to performance training.

THE NEED TO TRY THINGS OUT

Practice, application, and work in a shop or laboratory are necessary for the development of skills and the understanding of principles. If a new machine operator is expected to run equipment properly, he or she must have opportunities to operate the machine under carefully guided, controlled conditions. The aircraft mechanic who inspects, services or repairs a 747 should have plenty of prior practice in inspecting, troubleshooting, and repairing. The need for success in real situations dictates the need for tryout experiences before the real one takes place.

The importance of practice is obvious. Only by trainees having sufficient tryouts in simulated conditions can they be expected to produce maximumally when they are on the job. Therefore, performance tests are significant experiences in effective employee learning. In addition, performance tests warrant a great deal of attention from the instructor to make them vital, important, and seem realistic. They demand that the instructor give considerable attention to organizing, preparing, and conducting performance evaluations.

There are several problems relative to creating behavioral objectives for performance evaluation:

1. Identifying the specific desired behavior of the learner.
2. Specifying the statements that describe how the desired behavior is to be demonstrated.
3. Describing the desired behavior in a sufficiently precise manner so that misinterpretation is avoided.
4. Specifying or describing the conditions under which the terminal behavior is to be demonstrated.
5. Identifying the criteria to be met for an acceptable level of performance.
6. Agreeing through independent observation on the minimal level of acceptable behavior.

PLANNING FOR PERFORMANCE APPLICATION AND EVALUATION

The performance phase of learning cannot be isolated from all other phases (see illustration). It involves motivating, presenting, explaining, and evaluating. Each is important if the guidance of the trainee's activity is to lead to the effective development of skills and application of principles.

Plan the Physical Environment

The learning environment may be a shop bench for drilling and riveting skills or it may be the cockpit of jet aircraft for ejection seat checkout procedures. In any case, the instructor must make special efforts in planning to have all equipment, tools, manuals, or special devices ready for use by each trainee when it is needed. Everything must be as realistic and lifelike as possible.

Plan Trainee Assignments

A well-organized assignment sheet is an invaluable aid in scheduling trainees, equipment, tools, and time. Plan to rotate trainees in job-related various tasks so they become proficient in all of them, not just one or two. The instructor must see to it that trainees understand the relationship of the parts to the complete task. What or how much constitutes a complete task must be decided for each situation. No one formula is applicable to all. The instructor must select assignments within the range of the skill being taught.

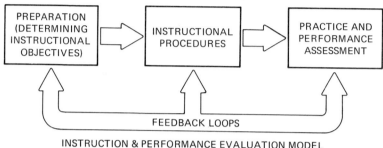

INSTRUCTION & PERFORMANCE EVALUATION MODEL

Instruction and Performance Evaluation Model

Plan to Control Practice

Controlled practice is defined as instruction or evaluation that provides careful, step-by-step learning under the direct supervision of an instructor. It consists of four phases.

1. *Explanation and demonstration by the instructor.* The introduction of the trainees to the skill to be acquired must contain the training objectives as well as the reasons for learning the skill. Each step must be explained and demonstrated from the trainee's point of view and so that each one can see and hear well.

    a. Describe precise actions required.
    b. Demonstrate so that all can see and hear well.
    c. Ask questions of the trainees.
    d. Insure the trainees understanding.
    e. Show the trainees all the actions necessary to perform the skill accurately and completely.

2. *Imitation and practice by the trainee.* The instructor must talk each trainee through the performance of each step of the task, correcting errors immediately and reinforcing correct behavior.

    a. Require each trainee to perform the skill.
    b. Allow enough time for the activity to become meaningful.

       Note: Be patient and avoid giving unnecessary help.

3. *Instructor supervision and correction of errors.* At the beginning of this

phase, the instructor should restate the training objectives so that the trainees will know the proficiency they must develop while practicing. During each individual practice session, the instructor must indicate to the trainees what to do should they need help and reinforce correct performance to build confidence in each trainee, asking questions on key points to check trainee understanding.

    a. Help trainees to improve and perfect performance.
    b. Correct errors as they occur.

> *Important:* Close supervision is important because some trainees will forget, some trainees learn slower than others, and some trainees will not have paid attention.

    4. *Evaluation.* This is the performance test phase. Skill proficiency level should not be evaluated until the trainees inform the instructor they are ready to be tested. The instructor should check the trainees' understanding by asking questions. While trainees are performing the test, the instructor must observe closely in order to identify mistakes. Training is effective only if the trainees are able to perform the assigned tasks according to the standards specified in the objectives. The performance test is the tool for determining whether the trainees have mastered the training objective.

    a. Judge trainee performance.
    b. Determine the effectiveness of instruction.
    c. Validate testing materials and procedures.

In this practice and imitation method, immediate application is a great advantage to learning. The fact that all the trainees are doing enables the instructor to evaluate the results of training. Practice skill requires close supervision; no matter how thorough the explanation and the demonstration, some trainees forget, some learn slower than others, and some will not have paid attention. The chief disadvantage of this type of instruction and evaluation is that it is time-consuming and can require many training aids and devices. In addition, safety precautions must be stressed, since there is always a danger of personal injury during shop or laboratory training.

USE A PROGRESS CHART

The successful completion of performance projects provides the trainee with a sense of accomplishment. Successful completions can be recorded on a progress chart (see illustration). This type of display ensures control of the instructional situation and indicates to trainees where they stand in relation to one another in the group.

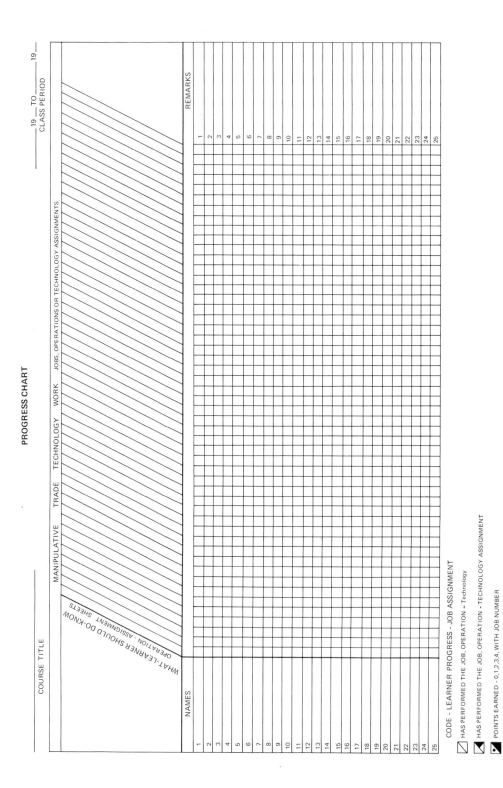

PROGRESS CHART

THE PERFORMANCE TEST

Suitable performance tests can be designed by setting up situations similar to the actual jobs the trainee was taught to do. Such tests must be typical of on-the-job performance, with identical standards. Performance tests can be designed for different types of learning, such as:

1. Manual skills—writing, typing, drilling, riveting, operating a loom, use of machines and tools.
2. Mental skills—speed-reading, human relations skill (cooperation, courtesy), malfunction analysis, troubleshooting.

In these tests, trainees are required to perform all or part of a job for which they have been trained, involving activities like assembly, disassembly, repair, identification or operating procedures. Performance tests can measure the quality of the finished job, skill and accuracy in operation, speed and ability to plan work, or the identification of parts.

The primary advantage of performance tests is that they are one of the best means of improving learner ability, because failures can be objectively observed and be used as the basis for further practice. Performance tests identify the weak spots that need more practice. They take advantage of the following laws of learning:

1. The Law of Readiness—People learn best when they are ready to learn; no one learns much who sees no reason for learning.
2. The Law of Exercise—The things that are repeated most often are the ones remembered best; they form the basis of practice and drill.
3. The Law of Effect—Learning is strengthened when it is accompanied by a pleasant and satisfying feeling; learning is weakened when it is associated with an unpleasantness.
4. The Law of Primacy—First impressions are often strong and unshakable; this means the instructor must be right the first time.
5. The Law of Intensity—A vivid, dramatic, or exciting learning experience teaches more than a routine or boring one.

> *Note:* A good performance test requires detailed planning and extensive preparation; it results in greater economy of time and materials.

ADMINISTERING THE PERFORMANCE TEST

The primary objective of performance and application testing is good performance. Performance testing cannot proceed in an orderly manner without continuous observation and evaluation. Oral critiques and discussion of the good and bad aspects of performance must be aimed at improved results in succeeding attempts. Without guidance in the analysis of mistakes, trainees may repeat tasks many times without mastering them. The instructor must insure the inclusion of a new experience in each repeated performance. Such new experiences can aid trainees in the elimination of old errors.

Practice does not necessarily mean that the identical steps must be repeated each time. Very often, the same principles can be applied to a variety of problems or situations. Practice for the trainee, then, becomes a matter of doing the task, diagnosing the errors made or the difficulties encountered, clarifying the why of the errors, then repeating the task in light of the corrections made.

Good performance evaluations contain no secrets as to what is to be checked or inspected. The trainees and the instructor must be in agreement on what is wanted, what qualities are to be judged, rated, or inspected, frequency of performance, and what standards are being used. Diagnosis by the instructor should be frequent without long delays between checks. When trouble shows up, it must be caught right away so as to head off further difficulties. Telling a trainee that he or she failed or missed or did not perform correctly is of some help. If the critique is accompanied by an analysis of the reasons why, the trainee is helped more effectively and long lastingly.

Trainees can often profit from suggested improvements to other trainees. This process is beneficial only after the instructor has developed a group of fast learners who can assist the slower ones. This also assists the better trainees, because they gain even better mastery themselves when they act as assistant instructors.

> *Caution:* If overdone, the use of trainees as assistant instructors can lead to the blind leading the blind.

The following are general considerations in conducting all types of performance evaluations.

1. Trainees must be motivated to perform. Learning results during the performance evaluation phase when trainee understanding of the principles taught is developed by effective instructional techniques and when the trainees are motivated to put those principles into practice.

2. Insure that practice does make perfect. Trainees on the job perform about as well as they do in training; therefore, the instructor must insure that trainee performance is perfected during the practical exercises of the training program.

3. Keep achievement standards progressive. In initial application tests or exercises, trainees should perform each step thoroughly and accurately under close supervision; the standards should be raised progressively on succeeding tests, with less assistance given.

4. Keep conditions realistic. Keep the conditions of the performance test

or exercise similar to those encountered on the job. In the initial exercises, however, it is more important to provide ideal conditions than to insist on absolute realism. It is most important that trainees learn to perform correctly; therefore, realistic conditions can be introduced for subsequent tests or exercises.

5. Procedures, principles, or skills must be tested as taught. Perfection is achieved through practice and performance testing only if trainees progress through the right movements, procedures, skills, or principles; the instructor must insure that the tests and exercises coincide with what has been taught.

6. Each step should be tested before moving to the next. Do not test too many operations, procedures, principles, tasks, or skills at any one time. Introduce a few activities, provide for adequate practice, review and critique the things taught, and examine or test the trainee's performance; then, when proficiency has been demonstrated, proceed to the next point or step.

7. Constant management of the learning environment is imperative. The fact that trainees are busy is not a guarantee that learning is taking place. During performance evaluation, the instructor must insure an affirmative answer to these questions:

a. Do the trainees know the what, why, and how of the activity?
b. Does the activity contribute to realization of the objectives?
c. Is maximum use being made of the equipment and instructional materials?
d. Are trainees being tested as taught?
e. Was ample time provided for the completion of the performance test?
f. Are safety measures being observed?
g. Are each of the performance valuations job related?

Important: A good performance test is a challenge in itself. Do not include unnecessary information that may lead trainees astray or force them to waste time on matters not related to the objectives or on-the-job performance.

A SAMPLE PERFORMANCE TEST

Title: Circuit Tracing and Hook-up Test.

Purpose of the test: To determine the accuracy with which trainees can perform circuit tracing and hook-up tasks.

The job: To trace circuits by ringing them out with a low-voltage buzzer preparatory to connecting a start-stop push-button switch for operating a magnetic controller, which in turn, connects the motor across the line.

Tasks:

1. Identification of controller terminals.

2. Identification of leads connecting the motor to the controller.
3. Identification of lines between the pushbutton and the controller.
4. Identification of the pushbutton terminals.

Time required per trainee: A trial run on the tasks indicates that each trainee should take no longer than 12 minutes. With time allowed for restoring gear, checking scores, etc., the test time for each trainee is 15 minutes. The equipment available allows six trainees to be tested at one time; 24 trainees can be tested each hour.

Organization of equipment:

1. Three start-stop pushbutton switches are mounted on a wall panel.
2. Circuit diagrams posted above panel.
3. Tools: Portable buzzers with leads attached. Chalk for marking terminals.

Assistance needed: Two instructors, one to act as timekeeper and one to supervise and score the trainees' work.

Scheduling: These tests are to be run in conjunction with the regular shopwork of the trainees. Six trainees are to be drawn from the shop class at 15-minute intervals and given the test. The remaining trainees in the class continue with their regular shop assignments. This procedure will insure that all trainees are kept busy and will prevent observation of the testing procedures by those not engaged in taking the tests.

Instructor information: Each trainee is to trace out the circuits and prepare to connect a Start-stop pushbutton switch to operate a magnetic controller that connects the motor across the line (two assists are allowed).

	Points
1. Identification of controller terminals (total of 4 terminals)	4
2. Identification of leads connecting the motor to the controller	3
3. Identification of the line between the pushbutton and the controller	4
4. Identification of pushbutton terminals	4
Total	15

Test instructions to trainees: You have 12 minutes to take this test. Trace out the circuits with a low-voltage buzzer. Mark each terminal in accordance with the lettering and numbering on the circuit diagram. Use chalk to mark each terminal. Scoring is based on the number of terminals corrrectly marked, so be as accurate and careful as possible. Work on your own equipment. Steady work without hurry will get you through the test in good time.

You are not to begin until the signal is given. At the end of 12 minutes the signal to stop will be given. If you finish before your time is up, do not move from your station to examine your neighbor's work. Wait until your work is checked and scored, then store all gear back in its original position and condition. Please remove all chalk marks.

SUMMARY

There are many advantages to performance testing.

- It is based on the psychological principle of learning by doing.
- Performance and repetition (the law of exercise) increases skills; skills bring satisfaction (the law of effect).
- With it demonstrations can be made dramatic and experience can be vivid (the law of intensity).
- Tests become more interesting and therefore motive better (the law of readiness).
- It allows trainees to progress at a measurable and realistic rate.
- Learning is likely to be rapid and lasting because of mental and motor-skill practice.
- Supervision of performance assists the trainee in acquiring correct procedures early (the law of primacy).
- It provides excellent feedback for the instructor to evaluate trainee learning and the effectiveness of the instruction.

The disadvantages of performance testing are that it:

- Takes more time than just telling.
- Is difficult to apply with large groups when individuals cannot see or cannot perform under close supervision.

Some hints for conducting performance tests are:

1. Motivate trainees to *do.*
2. Insure that practice makes perfect.
3. Keep achievement standards progressive.
4. Make the test conditions realistic.
5. Apply and test the material as taught.
6. Make each step move to the next.

10 Administering and Reporting Training Evaluation

Upon completion of the formal training activities, the overall effectiveness of the training must be evaluated. There are five specific areas to be checked:

1. The participant's *reaction.*
2. The *knowledge* and *skill* that were gained.
3. The *behaviors* that were acquired or changed.
4. The *results* as reflected in on-the-job performance.
5. The *reaction of the participant's supervisor* to the training.

EVALUATING TRAINEE REACTION

In following up on individual job training, it is relatively easy to determine the trainee's reaction. Did the employee enjoy the training sessions? Was enthusiasm obvious? Was effort put forth to learn quickly and perform well? It is realized that these are subjective questions, and so the answers will be somewhat subjective. But it is important that the questions be answered for they indicate how well the training staff did their job. Granted, the purpose of training is not to entertain the employee. But if the training is useful and interesting, the training department will be more effective.

Determining participant reaction to group sessions is somewhat more difficult. Nevertheless, when a training session is to be conducted several times, trainee reaction should be checked so that future sessions can be improved, if necessary. Trainee reaction to group training sessions is often measured by means of a questionnaire. A summary of the completed questionnaires is then compiled and used by the trainer to modify and improve the session. Sample questionnaires are presented in Figures 10–1 through 10–3.

1. Circle your overall reaction to the training session just completed:
    Very good   Good   Fair   Poor
2. How well did the material presented relate to your job?
    Completely   Quite a bit   Some   Very little
3. Will you be able to use the material presented in your daily duties?
    Frequently   Sometimes   Rarely   Never
4. Please evaluate the way the instructor presented the session.
    Very good   Good   Fair   Poor
5. How do you rate the visual aids that were used?
    Very good   Good   Fair   Poor
6. What are your suggestions for improving the session?

Fig. 10–1. Training Session Questionnaire.

A company's upper management, as well as a few training administrators, are interested in the trainees' reaction to the instructor, and so they ask the participants to evaluate the instructor. Sample evaluation forms are given in Figs. 10–4 and 10–5.

The training director must be *personally* aware of how well the programs and the staff members are performing. A good manager must determine whether the training department and staff offers the best type of course or program possible using the resources available. To do this, personal evaluations must be made, and the results found must become an integral part of the training director's program of staff development. The evaluation form shown in Fig. 10–6 may prove helpful in this regard.

EVALUATING TRAINEE KNOWLEDGE

Determining what a trainee has learned is usually accomplished through some form of test. It may be a verbal test, with the trainer quizzing the trainee. The trainee may be asked to perform the newly acquired skills, or

Course Title _____

Begin Date _____ End Date _____

Remarks (Optional)

Course Length
_____ About right   _____
_____ Too short   _____
_____ Too long   _____

Subject Coverage
_____ About right   _____
_____ Too little   _____
_____ Too much   _____

Handouts
_____ About right   _____
_____ Too few   _____
_____ Too many   _____

Use of Visual Aids
_____ Adequate   _____
_____ Too little   _____
_____ Too much   _____

Facilities (Classroom, rest rooms, eating areas, parking, etc.)
_____ Adequate   _____
_____ Could be improved   _____
                           _____

Rate the course as a whole (circle one)

   Excellent   Very good   Good   Fair   Poor

Was there anything in particular that you would like to comment upon?

_____
_____
_____

General Remarks:

_____
_____
_____

Fig. 10-2. Training Program Evaluation.

Course Title _____

Period of Training From _____   Through _____

Training Location _____

	Unsatisfactory	Poor	Satisfactory	Good	Excellent	Directions: Clear, concise, and constructive comments are required for each evaluation.
						Comments and Remarks
Course Length						
Course Introduction						
Main Presentation						
Theory						
Technical Level						
Continuity						
Comprehension						
Student Participation						
Course Review						
Number of Quizzes						
Quality of Quizzes						
Number of Study Periods						
Classrooms and Facilities						
Weight	0	1	2	3	4	
Total	0					

Name: _____   Date: _____

Fig. 10–3. Training Program Evaluation.

INSTRUCTOR EVALUATION FORM

INSTRUCTOR	TOPIC	DATE	TIME

A RATING OF (5) REPRESENTS THE HIGHEST POSSIBLE, A RATING OF (1) THE LOWEST

	ITEM	1	2	3	4	5	REMARKS
PRESENTATION	1. INTRODUCTION						
	2. EXPLANATION						
	3. ORDERLY						
	4. EMPHASIS ON KEY POINTS						
	5. QUESTIONS						
	6. APPLICATION ACTIVITY						
	7. SUMMARY TECHNIQUE						
INSTRUCTOR	8. APPEARANCE						
	9. EYE CONTACT						
	10. VOCABULARY						
	11. VOLUME						
	12. CLARITY						
	13. SPEED/PACE						
	14. GESTURES						
TRAINING AIDS	15. ACCURACY IN PRINCIPLE						
	16. LEGIBILITY						
	17. TIE-IN EXPLANATION						
	18. DID THEY AID TEACHING?						
GENERAL	19. ROOM ENVIRONMENT						
	20. SUPERVISION AND CONTROL						
	21. KNOWLEDGE OF SUBJECT						
	22. SAFETY						
	23. OVERALL INSTRUCTOR RATING						

ADDITIONAL SUGGESTIONS:
(USE BACK SIDE OF SHEET IF NECESSARY)

_____
EVALUATOR

Fig. 10-4. Instructor Evaluation Form.

INSTRUCTOR EVALUATION

NAME		DATE		TIME
EVALUATOR	COURSE		SUBJECT	

A RATING OF (1) REPRESENTS THE HIGHEST POSSIBLE, A RATING OF (5) THE LOWEST

ITEM	1	2	3	4	5	COMMENTS OR SUGGESTIONS
INTRODUCTION						
ADAPTATION TO GROUP'S LEVEL						
QUESTIONING TECHNIQUE						
TRAINEE PARTICIPATION						
GROUP'S INTEREST						
ORGANIZATION OF MATERIAL						
KNOWLEDGE OF SUBJECT MATTER						
USE OF TRAINING AIDS						
SUMMARY						
EYE CONTACT						
VOCABULARY						
CLARITY						
SPEED/PACE OF DELIVERY						
GESTURES						
GROOMING						
TACT						
ENTHUSIASM						
ROOM ENVIRONMENT						
LESSON PLAN						
OBJECTIVES						

Fig. 10-5. Instructor Evaluation.

EVALUATION REPORT FOR CLASSROOM INSTRUCTORS

INSTRUCTOR'S NAME:	DATE
TOPIC	

INSTRUCTIONAL SKILLS & CLASSROOM MANAGEMENT	UNSATIS-FACTORY	NEEDS IMPROVE-MENT	SATIS-FACTORY	ABOVE AVERAGE	SUPERIOR
1. KNOWLEDGE OF SUBJECT MATTER					
2. DEVELOPMENT AND USE OF EFFECTIVE INSTRUCTIONAL TECHNIQUES					
3. EFFECTIVE PARTICIPANT EVALUATION					
4. PROVISION FOR INDIVIDUAL DIFFERENCES AMONG PARTICIPANTS					
5. VARIATION IN MATERIALS AND TEACHING TECHNIQUES					
6. CONSISTENT AND CAREFUL PLANNING IN ACCORDANCE WITH OBJECTIVES AND LESSON PLAN					
7. ORGANIZATION AND EFFECTIVE DIRECTION OF TRAINING ACTIVITIES					
8. ABILITY TO MAINTAIN GOOD CLASS CONTROL					
9. RAPPORT WITH PARTICIPANTS					
10. PHYSICAL CLASSROOM ENVIRONMENT — VENTILATION, HEAT, LIGHT					
11. INSTRUCTIONAL CLASSROOM ENVIRONMENT — VALUABLE & PLEASANT SURROUNDINGS					
12.					

COMMENT:

PERSONAL CHARACTERISTICS	UNSATIS-FACTORY	NEEDS IMPROVE-MENT	SATIS-FACTORY	ABOVE AVERAGE	SUPERIOR
1. GROOMING AND GENERAL APPEARANCE					
2. APPARENT PHYSICAL HEALTH AND ENERGY					
3. APPARENT EMOTIONAL AND SOCIAL ADJUSTMENT					
4. INTEREST AND ENTHUSIASM ABOUT WORK					
5. USE OF GOOD JUDGMENT					
6. VOICE AND SPEECH					
7.					

COMMENT:

Fig. 10-6. Evaluation Report for Classroom Instructors.

PROFESSIONAL ATTITUDES AND GROWTH	UNSATIS-FACTORY	NEEDS IMPROVE-MENT	SATIS-FACTORY	ABOVE AVERAGE	SUPERIOR
1. OBSERVANCE OF ETHICS OF THE TRAINING PROFESSION					
2. EFFORT MADE TO IMPROVE CLASSROOM METHODS AND TECHNIQUES					
3. RESPONSE TO SUPERVISION AND SUGGESTIONS FOR IMPROVEMENT					
4. RELATIONSHIP WITH OTHER DEPARTMENTAL PERSONNEL					
5. WILLINGNESS TO SHARE IN ALL TRAINING RESPONSIBILITIES					
6. PROMPTNESS AND ACCURACY WITH REPORTS					
7. CONFORMANCE WITH AUTHORIZED POLICIES AND PROCEDURES					
8.					
COMMENT:					

INTERPERSONAL RELATIONSHIPS	UNSATIS-FACTORY	NEEDS IMPROVE-MENT	SATIS-FACTORY	ABOVE AVERAGE	SUPERIOR
1. RELATIONSHIP WITH OTHERS					
2. PARTICIPATION IN TRAINING AND EDUCATION RELATED ORGANIZATIONS					
3. EFFECTIVENESS IN INTERPRETING THE TRAINING PROGRAMS AND ACTIVITIES					
4.					
COMMENT:					

GENERAL EVALUATION

CONSIDERING TOTAL EFFECTIVENESS IN THE TRAINING PROGRAMS, I BELIEVE THIS INSTRUCTOR SHOULD BE RATED:

5 UNSATISFACTORY	4 NEEDS IMPROVEMENT	3 SATISFACTORY	2 ABOVE AVERAGE	1 SUPERIOR

I FEEL THAT THE POSSIBILITY OF MEETING THE DEPARMENT'S STANDARDS IS:

POOR	QUESTIONABLE	FAIR	GOOD	EXCELLENT

TRAINING DIRECTOR'S SIGNATURE

INSTRUCTOR'S SIGNATURE*

*THIS SIGNATURE INDICATES THAT THE INSTRUCTOR AND TRAINING DIRECTOR TOGETHER DISCUSSED THIS REPORT. IT DOES NOT NECESSARILY DENOTE AGREEMENT WITH ALL FACTORS OF THE EVALUATION.

DATE OF CONFERENCE WITH INSTRUCTOR

Fig. 10–6. Evaluation Form for Classroom Instructors (continued)

the evaluation may take one of the several written forms described previously. Examples are:

1. Essay questions
2. True or false
3. Multiple-choice
4. Matching
5. Fill in the blanks

The trainee is sometimes tested prior to training and then again afterward. The difference in performance indicates how much the trainee learned as a result of the training and provides the training staff with information as to how to further improve the program.

Do not test simply to see if the trainee remembers *everything* that was taught. The purpose of training was to teach the employee certain key concepts, methods, and techniques of doing a job. Therefore, the test must cover those points that are critical to success on the job. After all, that is what management really wants the employee to learn.

EVALUATING PERFORMANCE

Before employees attempt new procedures on their own, they should try them out under supervision, as follows:

1. The tryout performance consists of having trainees go through the operation of the job under the watchful eye of the instructor to make sure that each individual understands each step of the operation.
2. The performance evaluation also consists of questioning each individual in order to check their understanding of the facts about the job to be performed or their knowledge upon which judgment and decisions may be based.
3. During the tryout performance, the instructor must correct the trainee's mistakes calmly, patiently, and thoroughly. This is what good teaching and coaching is all about. Once the instructor believes that the trainee has a good grasp of the job, the trainee should be encouraged to proceed with the work alone. In addition, trainees should be encouraged to bring any questions and problems to the instructor.

Performance tryout and measurement consists of four major parts:

1. Have the trainee go through the job several times.
2. Explain the key points, and correct any mistakes.

3. Have the trainee do the job while the instructor watches.
4. Put the trainees on their own when they feel confident.

The following four steps should be used in evaluating performance:

1. *Trainee performs under an instructor's direction.*
   - In advance of any movement, the trainee tells what he is going to do, how he will do it, and then he does the step.
   - Don't rush the trainee.
   - Don't lose patience and take the work away from the trainee.
   - Don't confuse the trainee with too many directions.
   - Point out the things the trainee does right rather than dwell on those things that are done wrong. If the trainee forgets what to do or tries to do the wrong thing, stop him, and, by asking him questions, get him to review the instructions.
2. *Trainee performs without direction.*
   - The trainee performs the steps of procedure while the instructor looks on.
   - The trainee should work for accuracy first and then for speed.
   - This step should continue as long as time permits or until the trainee is working up to operation standards.
   - The instructor watches carefully for any bad habits or variations in procedure that might lead to faulty performance. If such habits or variations occur, the instructor should reteach that portion of the lesson.
3. *Practice on equipment.*
   - All trainees should have the opportunity to work on the equipment. If this is impossible, they should be given a training project to complete.
   - Whenever possible, use the "buddy system" during practice by placing two people at a time on a trainer or piece of equipment—one person as the operator and the other as the observer. If this is impossible due to limitation of training equipment, trainees might be assigned to work together on a training project.
4. *Class activities.*
   - While two people are working on the trainer or a piece of equipment, the rest of the class could:
     a. Review material covered to date (buddy system or a list of questions).
     b. Complete a worksheet on the equipment just covered (location of parts, function, etc.).
     c. Work out possible solutions to typical problems encountered when working on the equipment (problems supplied by instructor).

EVALUATING BEHAVIOR

Behavior, or how an employee performs the job, is best evaluated through personal observation. Recall how the employee performed prior to exposure to the training activities. Compare these performances with the behaviors following the training. If the behaviors have changed significantly, it is probably as a result of the training program conducted.

EVALUATING RESULTS

Since the training occurred, is the employee producing the expected quantity of work, at acceptable quality levels, within the prescribed time limits? If the results of the employee's performance agree with the training objectives that were set, the training has been successful. If the objectives are not being met, then the training administrator must take a second look at the training program, or the employee, or the training staff—or all three.

The primary objective of training activities is the results. However, they are not the only objective. To have a better understanding of the total picture, the training administrator must collect data concerning *knowledge* acquisition, *behavior* changes, and *reaction* to the instruction. For example, if the instructor receives unfavorable reactions from the trainees, they are probably paying more attention to what is bothering them than to the content of the training lesson. Therefore, the trainees are not learning as much as they could. So, *reaction* is important.

If an employee performs the job, the *knowledge* is there. But do they have *all* the necessary job knowledge? Are there key, even critical elements of the job that the trainee has not performed yet, and that will not arise for some time after training? When those situations arise, if employees fail to perform, what will be said? That they forgot? That they have a poor attitude? Or will the training director (or instructor) recognize that some of the information was never fully learned to begin with?

Employee *behavior* is also important. It is often the key to performance problems. Even though the employee may be achieving the *results* desired, the training staff should also be concerned with *how* the results are obtained. Poor work habits could be forming that could prove to be very troublesome in the future.

MANAGEMENT REACTION TO TESTING

While it is important to measure the trainees' reaction to training, it is also important for the training staff to determine management's reaction. The prime objective of training is to develop qualified employees. Training programs are conducted to bring to the employees those concepts, methods or techniques that are critical to success on the job. If the supervisors do not notice a change in employee on-the-job behavior, the entire training program may be in jeopardy. It is imperative that the training staff follow up by asking the trainees' supervisors if they notice a difference in job performance.

All the areas of evaluation should be checked to see if there is room for improvement in the training program. Evaluating these areas can help in deciding if all the training objectives have been met. On the other hand, if it is concluded that the objectives have not been met, everyone will want to know why the training fell short. The training staff must know how the training should be modified so that it can produce better results in the future.

EVALUATION OF THE EVALUATION

Suppose someone questions the validity of the tests being used in the training program. How could disagreements be reconciled? Empirical research may not provide a key. But all inquiries of validity must be based on a rational evaluation of the specific objectives of the training activities.

> *Note:* Technically correct items or grammatically correct items
> may not include an important idea that is worthwhile measuring.

If a test serves its intended function, it is said to be valid; if it does not, it is invalid. A test is valid only for specific functions under specifiable conditions and, generally, for a specific time and groups of learners. For example, an instructor might construct a test that was valid during one instructional cycle but not equally valid the next time the program was taught because of changes in the instructional material, the process, or the state of the art. Similarly, a particular test might be valid to a group of technicians but have little or no validity for supervisors or managers.

In determining the performance of the test items, the following steps are important considerations to check.

1. *Validity:* Did the test measure what it was designed to measure? Check the specific objectives.
2. *Reliability:* Did each test item measure with accuracy and consistency? Follow up on-the-job assists to determine this.
3. *Mechanical simplicity:* Was the test easy to give, easy to take, and easy to score? Instructors and trainees are working too hard if the answers are no.
4. *Discrimination:* Was there a reasonable distribution of scores (or items missed)? Did the average fall approximately at the center of the distribution curve?

Note: The word grade is not used in this step because grading employees is an individual company policy. The author does not recommend the grading of employees. Scores are used to check the quality of the test and the instruction. Task performance on the job is the key.

5. *Comprehensiveness:* Was there at least one test item on each key point covered in the instruction?
6. *Range of difficulty:* Did the test include some easy items, some items of medium difficulty, and some that were fairly difficult?
7. *Objectivity:* Was scoring affected by the opinions of the scorer? This is especially true for essay test items.

TEST AS A PREDICTOR

An important use of tests is to predict how individuals will perform or behave in certain situations. If a test is accurate in making these predictions, then it is valid in that sense. When a test is intended primarily to make a prediction, its validity depends on how successfully it estimates the learner's performance in a real-life situation. Trainers must look for predictors of how well trainees will perform on the job.

A test can never do a perfect job of predicting an outcome. Its success as a predictor depends entirely upon how well it correlates with some specific criteria of successful performance.

ASSESSMENT VALUE OF TESTS

The assessment function of a test is the evaluation of the effectiveness of a performance at a particular time—for example, when an instructor gives a test to measure the trainees' progress in a specific unit of instruction. The purpose of the test is not to predict what the learners will do in the future, but rather to measure their achievement to that point.

Both instructors and trainees tend to take test results too seriously. Much more important is the cumulative record of performance in the entire training program. Never accept a test at face value until some evidence is obtained to show that it does what it is purported to do. Although tests provide potentially hlepful information for many types of decisions, the two major functions of tests are:

1. The *prediction function* is an effort to accurately predict some important future behavior.
2. The *assessment function* is concerned with the performance of a

trainee in a specific unit of instruction or with the trainee's overall progress up to a particular point in time.

GOOD TEST ADMINISTRATION

A good test consists not only of a set of well-written items but also of a set of well-thought-out procedures and instructions that are clear to the test takers. Test instructions are a very important part of the testing procedure. It is advisable to go through a sample test item with the test takers before they begin. The instructor should:

1. Arrive at the classroom well in advance to make sure that the materials needed for the test are on hand, including a supply of sharpened pencils.
2. Save time by placing test and answer sheets on the desks or tables without waiting for all the test takers to be seated.
3. See that the testing room is well lighted and ventilated.
4. Make preliminary instructions so clear and easy to follow that confidence is established in the test takers. Without this confidence, they may be nervous and tense.
5. Explain what the test taker should do once the test has been completed.
6. Take whatever time is needed to clarify the test instructions.
7. If timing is important, place a large clock in the front of the room so that the test takers can see how much time has elapsed.
8. Announce and adhere to prescribed time limits for the test.
9. Follow a planned and understandable procedure throughout the testing period. The best procedures are gained through careful planning and preparation.
10. Avoid distractions, and should not overlook himself/herself as a source.

When reviewing test results, correct misunderstandings. Give explanations rather than just indicate the correct answers. Allow the trainees to make criticisms of the test items they did not understand.

The effectiveness of examinations depends on good administration. The test administrator is in a crucial position, and can "do" or "undo" a well-prepared training program . . . so, *be prepared.*

Testing Time

How much time should the instructor spend questioning or evaluating the trainees? The amount of time devoted to trainee evaluation is governed somewhat by the subject matter. If too much time is used for evaluation, time is lost from instruction. If too little time is spent on evaluation, neither the trainees nor the instructor will know if any progress is being made.

Frequency of Test

Oral questioning should be done frequently. In addition, it is better to have many short written tests than a few long ones. In short, sufficient questions or tests should be given so that the instructor knows at all times what progress the trainees are making.

Length of Tests

It is better to give many short tests. Trainees often feel defeated when tests are long, and so they become frustrated and fail. Therefore, *keep tests short.*

Representative Test Items

The material covered on a test must be representative of that given during the training activities. It is the instructor's responsibility to see to it that the training program objectives have been met. This is easy to accomplish if the test items are based upon the specific objectives for the needs of the training. There are no valid excuses for the trainees not being given an opportunity to learn the things for which they will be held accountable—on the test or on the job.

TEST DIRECTIONS

One of the characteristics of a good test is the formulation of a good set of test directions. Give complete instructions for taking the test. If references and aids may be used by the test taker, they must be listed. Explain the manner in which the test taker is to record answers. These instructions must always be given, even if it can be assumed that the test taker has had experience with similar tests.

There must be directions given for each type of test item stating clearly and concisely what the test taker is required to do, how to indicate the answer, and where to place the answer.

Example for true–false test items:

Directions: Listed below are a number of statements; some are true and some are false. If any part of a statement is false, the entire statement is false. Make your decision by circling T for true and F for false.

Example for multiple-choice test items:

Directions: Each of the incomplete statements or questions given below is followed by several possible alternatives (answers). Select the best answer for each test item. Indicate your selection by circling the number in front of it.

Example for matching test items:
Directions: The names in column I are identified by numbers; those in column II by letters. The task is to match or pair each number in column I with a letter in column II.

Example for completion test items:
Directions: Each of the numbered blank spaces in the following incomplete statements indicates an omitted word or words. Complete the meaning of each statement by writing the correct word(s) in the corresponding numbered blanks.

HOW TO TAKE A TEST

Many instructors in the business and industry community think of studying and test taking as being done primarily by students in high school or college. But the need for studying and good test taking habits does not end with formal education.

1. *Guidelines for studying.* Procrastination is the enemy of good study and work habits. Do not put off getting started on an assignment. See to it that the proper conditions for study exist (quiet, equipment, lighting). When studying, give the subject full attention. Take meaningful notes. Make it a habit to use reference books. It is important to avoid frustration when confronted with a difficult assignment. Do the studying and reviews on a day-to-day basis; this enhances retention of the material covered.

2. *Guidelines for test taking.* There is a technique to taking tests that pays great dividends when the instructor shares and explains the following:

a. Read over the entire test carefully. Are there specific instructions on how the answers should be prepared? Determine exactly what is wanted. Check the number of questions to be answered.
b. Answer first the question about which the most is known. Then the next easiest ones, and so on.

   Important: Do not waste time at first on the hard questions.

c. Do the scratch work on a separate sheet, if allowed. Arrange the required work on the answer sheet in a neat and orderly way.
d. Check all answers and work processes.
e. Reread the test paper. Check again what was asked for. Be sure to give what is wanted the way it was wanted.
f. If necessary ask the instructor for further clarification.

g. Pay no attention to others taking the test, especially those who leave early. Budget your time and use it all to check and recheck answers.

h. Do not leave any question unanswered. Put down the best answer you can.

Remember: Check the test paper before turning it in.

Many test failures are due to silly or careless mistakes. A systematic orderly, and calm approach to test taking can help in avoiding foolish errors. The tests should be prepared so that good and careful test takers can pass them. Quizzes must not be prepared with high built-in failure factors.

Most important: The test must be on points that are critical to success on the job.

11 _____A Final Note

The primary reasons for testing are to improve instruction and increase learning. Evaluation is concerned with the estimation of learning effectiveness. It is therefore inseparable from the learning process itself. The entire process begins with a clear definition of objectives, in which specific standards and sample test items are defined to serve as vehicles for estimating the effectiveness of individual trainees in the essential elements of the subject matter or job task being evaluated.

To be effective, the evaluation and testing process must be systematic and continuous. Ongoing examinations give instructors positive indications of how well the trainees are doing and how well they both are meeting the specific training objectives. In addition, repeated testing makes trainees more confident in the testing situation.

For tests to be most useful, the conclusions reached based on them must be presented in a form that can be properly interpreted by the instructor, the trainee, and company management. Whatever means are used, tests and resultant reports should possess the following characteristics:

1. Reliability: It should yield consistent results.
2. Validity: It should actually measure what it is supposed to and nothing else.

3. Objectivity: The personal viewpoint of the scorer should not affect the score achieved.
4. Comprehensiveness: It should provide a liberal sample of all material being measured.
5. Differentiation: It should detect relatively small differences between the levels of achievement of trainees.

How well each of the various styles or means of testing meets the requirements of these five characteristics is the acid test for choosing one means rather than another.

When examinations are being constructed, the desired specific change in behavior should be the most important thing being measured. Only observable behavior should be measured. Behaviors that result from learning include comparing, differentiating, contrasting, generalizing, explaining, and problem solving. The evaluation plan and test items should be based upon an appraisal of these factors.

- Analysis of how well the training and development objectives have been met.
- A determination of the effectiveness of the program and activities, as well as the personnel who conducted them.
- An evaluation of the instructional materials, methods, and techniques.
- An assessment of the change in trainee behavior.

In making evaluations, use:

- Oral test questions.
- Performance tests.
- Written test questions.

For the training evaluation process to be complete, it is necessary to evaluate the effectiveness of training programs. Is the training activity achieving its developmental goals? Training does not always train; sometimes it contributes to problems rather than solve them. An examination of the training itself can reveal failures attributable to:

- Use of the wrong teaching method.
- Poor instruction.
- Poorly prepared instruction.
- Conducting the training in the wrong learning environment.
- Trainee resistance to the training.
- Doing the wrong things right.

There must be a documentation of all the evidence for:

- Efficiency of the training activities.
- Trainee performance.
- Effectiveness in transfer to the job performance.
- Instructor and trainee reactions.
- Management reaction.
- The cost of development.

Simply stated: evaluation is a wide range of activities undertaken to determine the worth of something. The evaluation procedure should be based on an identification and appraisal.

For the training evaluation process to be complete, some effort should be made to determine the cost of learning by analyzing the relationship between the length of the job task to be learned and the costs involved in learning the task. Someone has to pay the cost of employee training and development. The training staff should be ready to answer questions as to the relevance of the developmental activities.

WHAT THIS BOOK IS ALL ABOUT

It is hoped that this text has been of some assistance in developing a well-rounded program of evaluation. The instructor and the trainee will want to know the answer to the following question: How am I doing? It is hoped that the contents of this book have assisted the reader in reaching an answer and in drawing the proper conclusions about training activities and the trainees participating in them.

> *Important:* Learning does not stop once the learner has finished preparation. The trainee continues to learn while taking a test. Because of this, *tests are teaching tools.*

Recommended
Readings

Abu-Sayf, F. K. and J. J. Diamond. "Effect of Confidence Level in Multiple-Choice Test Answers on Reliability and Validity of Scores." *Journal of Educational Research,* November 1976.

Ahmann, J. S. *Multiple-Choice Question: A Close Look.* Princeton, N.J.: Educational Testing Service, 1963.

Becker, S. P. "How To Measure Training Results In Your Organization." *Training,* April 1977.

Besco, Tiffin, & King, "Evaluation Techniques for Management Development Programs." *Journal of ASTD,* October 1959.

Bolen, J. E. "Dilemma in Evaluating Instruction." *The National Elementary Principal,* February, 1973.

Brody, W. and N. J. Powell. "A New Approach to Oral Testing." *Educational and Psychological Measurement,* Vol. 7.

Buchanan, P. C. "A System for Evaluating Supervisory Development Programs." *Personnel,* January 1955.

Caldwell, M. S. "An Approach to Assessment of Educational Planning." *Educational Technology.*

Chabotar, K. J. "The Logic of Training Evaluation." *Personnel,* July–August 1977.

Chase, C. I. "Classroom Testing and the Right to Privacy." *Phi Delta Kappan,* December 1976.

Denova, C. C. "Is This Any Way to Evaluate a Training Activity? You Bet It Is!" *Personnel Journal,* July 1968.

Denova, C. C. "Training Evaluating Causes Change in Behavior." *Personnel Administration,* September–October 1969.

Diederich, P. B. "Cooperative Preparation and Rating of Essay Tests." *English Journal,* Vol. 56, 1967.

Doe, B. "Don't Ask Too Much of the Tester." *The Times (London) Educational Supplement,* August 30, 1974.

Downey, G. W. "Is It Time We Started Teaching Children How to Take Tests?" *American School Board Journal,* January 1977.

Ebel, R. L. "Can Teachers Write Good True-False Test Items?" *Journal of Educational Measurement,* Spring 1975.

Elliott, V. L. "Peer Evaluation for Teachers? Why Not?" *Elementary English,* May 1974.

Follman, J. "Relationship Between Objective Test Formats." *Educational Review,* February 1974.

Goodacre, D. M. "The Experimental Evaluation of Management Training: Principles and Practice." *Personnel,* May 1957.

Gronlund, N. E. *Stating Behavioral Objectives for Classroom Instruction.* London: Macmillan, 1970.

Helms, W. C. "Shop Supervisors Evaluate Supervisory Training," *Journal of ASTD,* January–February 1955.

Hughes, H. H. and W. E. Trimble. "The Use of Complex Alternatives in Multiple-Choice Items." *Educational and Psychological Measurement,* Vol. 25.

Howe, C. and A. R. Elsbree. "An Evaluation of Training in Three Acts." *Training and Development Journal,* July–September 1977.

Jensen, A. R. "Test Bias and Construct Validity." *Phi Delta Kappan,* December 1976.

Kirkpatrick, D. L. "How to Start an Objective Evaluation of Your Training Program." *Journal of ASTD,* May–June 1956.

Kirkpatrick, D. L. "Techniques for Evaluating Training Programs." *Journal of ASTD,* November 1959.

Lacroix, W. J. "Evaluating Learner Growth." *Man/Society/Technology,* February 1974.

LaFave, L. "Essay vs. Multiple-Choice: Which Test Is Preferable?" *Psychology in the Schools,* March 1966.

MacCullough, A. V. "Evaluation of Executive Training Courses." *The Controller,* May 1954.

McDermott, F. A. "What It Takes to Make Training Pay Off." *Supervisory Management,* May 1964.

Mahler, W. "Evaluation of Management Development Programs." *Personnel,* September 1953.

Moffie, Calhoon, "Evaluation of a Management Development Program." *Personnel Psychology,* Winter 1964.

Murdick, R. G., "Measuring the Profit in Industry Training Programs." *Journal of ASTD,* April 1960.

Norman, J. H. "Dollars and Cents Evaluation of a Training Program." *Journal of ASTD,* October 1959.

Patterson, J. L. "How to Avoid the Dangers of Testing." *The National Elementary Principal,* July 1975.

Siro, E. "Performance Tests and Objective Observation." *Industrial Arts and Vocational Education,* Vol. 32.

Stoker, H. W. and R. P. Kropp. "Measurement of Cognitive Process." *Journal of Educational Measurement,* January 1964.

Storey, A. G. "Review of Evidence or the Case Against the True-False Item." *Journal of Educational Research,* Vol. 59.

Thorley, S. "Evaluating an In-Company Management Training Program." *Training and Development Journal,* September 1969.

Viteless, M. S., "Evaluation of a Program of Humanistic Studies for Executives." *Personnel Psychology,* Spring 1959.

Weisbros, B. A. "Conceptual Issues in Evaluating Training Programs." *Monthly Labor Review,* October 1966.

Wesman, A. G. and G. K. Bennett. "The Use of 'None of These' as an Option in Test Construction." *Journal of Educational Psychology,* Vol. 37.

Wotruba, T. R. and P. L. Wright. "How to Develop a Teacher-Rating Instrument." *Journal of Higher Education,* November 1975.

Index